The Sentiments of Philo Judeus Concerning the Logos, or, Word of God

THE
SENTIMENTS
OF
PHILO JUDEUS

CONCERNING THE

ΛΟΓΟΣ, or WORD of GOD;

TOGETHER WITH

LARGE EXTRACTS FROM HIS WRITINGS

COMPARED WITH THE SCRIPTURES

ON MANY OTHER

PARTICULAR AND ESSENTIAL DOCTRINES

OF THE CHRISTIAN RELIGION.

By JACOB BRYANT.

CAMBRIDGE,

PRINTED BY JOHN BURGES PRINTER TO THE
UNIVERSITY;

AND SOLD BY J. DEIGHTON, CAMBRIDGE;
MESSRS. CADELL & DAVIES, P. ELMSLEY,
AND T. PAYNE, LONDON.

MDCCXCVII.

JAN 1

PREFACE.

As a variety of prejudices prevail in the world in refpect to the Chriftian Religion, fome againft it in general, and others againft it's particular doctrines, it is very providential, that we have on the other hand an equal variety of evidences to counteract the Evil, and remedy it's confequences. The early Fathers fhew plainly, what was in their time the Doctrine and Faith of the Church. Nor have there been wanting in our own nation excellent Writers, by whom our Holy Religion has been vindicated, and it's Doctrines maintained. Yet the common-place argument is ftill urged, that they, who have embraced a fyftem, will fupport it, and thofe, who get by the Image, will certainly uphold the fhrine.

The

PREFACE.

The most unexceptionable assurances
must therefore be those, which are afforded
by a person perfectly neutral: one, who
has no predilection, and who is open to
no other influence, but that of Truth.
Philo, the learned Jew, with whom I shall
be principally concerned, stands precisely
in this happy predicament. He lived in
the time of our Saviour, and survived him
long: he was conversant with many of his
Disciples; and, as we are informed, with
some of the Apostles. From his situation
he had an opportunity of seeing the early
progress of Christianity, and of being acquainted with it's Doctrines: and of this
knowledge he gives us abundant proof, as
will be hereafter shewn. At the same time
the Religion, in which he had been edu-
cated, and to which he was firmly devoted,
takes off all suspicion of prejudice from
every thing, which he advances. Indeed,
he may be looked upon, not merely as

neutral

neutral, but in fome degree as hoftile. For though he appears to be fo far affected, by what he had learned of Chriftianity, as to adopt many of it's principal Articles, yet he was far from having any regard to it, as a Syftem; nor did he fhew any refpect to it's Author. He never once makes mention of either of them. His evidence therefore in refpect to the Doctrines, which he has tranfmitted, is the moft unexceptionable, that can poffibly be required; and obviates all the imputations of prejudice, which caprice and folly have framed. This argument is fo clear, and of fuch confequence, that, I hope, I fhall be excufed, if in the courfe of this Treatife I prefent it more than once to the Reader, that it may be continually in his view. In whatever Philo has advanced to our prefent purpofe, he was influenced folely by the force of reafon and truth. And wonderful muft thofe Truths have been, which could procure the

r Tent

affent of one, who has taken not the leaft notice of their Author, and probably held him in contempt.

It muft be confeffed, that this Platonic Philofopher was in general addicted to myftery and refinement. But in the Articles, which he borrowed from Chriftianity, he is perfectly clear and precife, and his teftimony is paft controverfy valid. Great advantage may therefore be obtained from his Evidence; as fome very learned and ingenious Writers have lately obferved, and indeed fo far proved, that any farther profecution of the Subject might be deemed unneceffary. But as there is a path, I think, ftill left open and unexplored, I have ventured to follow it's direction; ftriving, if poffible, to add to thofe advantages, which accrue from thofe learned Writers.

As

As the moſt curious and intereſting Article, upon which Philo dwells, is the nature of the Logos, or DIVINE WORD, I ſhall commence with his Evidence upon that head; only premiſing the notions of the firſt Innovators in Religion, who were of his time, or immediately followed.

———————

I cannot conclude this Preface without returning my ſincereſt Thanks to the Gentlemen of the Syndicate at Cambridge, for their repeated goodneſs in permitting this Treatiſe, after a former, to be printed at the Univerſity preſs.

J. B.

CYPENHAM, January 3, 1797.

PHILO JUDEUS.

PART I.

PROÆM.

OUR Saviour, while he was upon earth, gave an account of himself, and of his miffion; and difplayed the high character, which he bore: and this after his death was confirmed by his Apoftles. From thefe evidences we find, that he was the Son of God, both God, and Man; confequently of two natures, human, and divine. He accordingly juft before his afcenfion gave his laft mandate to his Apoftles, that they fhould go, and inftruct all nations, —

A
baptizing

baptizing them in the name of the Father, and of the Son, and of the Holy Ghost.[1] Hence we find, that he introduced himself, and confequently ranked himfelf with God, the Creator, and Lord of the univerfe; a degree of eminence, which no man, nor any created being, however high and excellent, could have dared to affume. At the fame time we are told, that he was born of a Virgin, and appeared in the humble form of a man; and was, as we are taught, and commanded to believe, perfect God, and perfect Man.

Thefe arguments, and many more to the fame purpofe, have been ufed by pious and learned men, by which the faith of the world in general has been confirmed: and they may feem unneceffary to be introduced again. But I have been obliged to repeat, what has been faid above; as many have fallen off: and it is my purpofe to fhew the mode of their deviation; and the extremes into which they have run.

[1] Matth. xxviii. 19.

OF THE CONTRARIETY AND INCONSISTENCE
WHICH HAS PREVAILED.

Hence we may perceive, how wayward and excentrick men are at different times; and how inconfiftent in their opinions. We now try to fet afide the divinity of Chrift; and he is by fome reduced to the ftate of an angel, by others he is efteemed a prophet, by others he is rated as a mere man. But it was not fo of old, in the firft ages of Chriftianity. Many of thofe, who feceded from the infant church, deviated the contrary way. They allowed the divine nature, but denied the human. For the miracles of Chrift were fo well attefted, and at the fame time fo wonderfully difplayed, that they could not believe, that they were the operation of man. Some of thefe lived in the days of the very Apoftles; and others in the enfuing century: fo that they had no doubt about the operations. But they abufed their faith; and would not allow that they were effected by any human power.

Thus

Thus the manhood of Chrift was denyed then, as his divinity is now.

This falling off was not unforefeen; and feems to have been continually obviated by our Saviour. Though he declared to the world, that he was the Son of God, and came from his Father; yet he ftrongly and repeatedly inculcates, that he was alfo the Son of man. It is accordingly faid,—[1] *The fon of man goeth.* [2] *The fon of man fhall come in his glory.* [3] *The fon of man fhall be three days and three nights in the heart of the earth.* [4] *The fon of man muft be lifted up. The fon of man muft fuffer.* [5] *The fon of man is delivered into the hands of wicked men.* [6] *The foxes have holes, and the birds of the air nefts; but the fon of man hath not where to lay his head.* [7] *Judas, betrayeft thou the fon of man with a kifs?*

It is remarkable, that after the death of our

---

[1] Matt. xxvi. 24. [2] Matt. xxv. 31. [3] Matt. xii. 40. [4] John iii. 14. [5] Mark ix. 31. [6] Luke ix. 58.
Luke xii. 48.

our Saviour, the Apoftles never make ufe of
thefe terms, nor call him any longer the
[1] Son of man. As he was now received
into glory, and become the Lord of life,
they fpeak of him in a different manner.
However, when there is occafion, they never
fail to infift upon his human nature. It is
therefore ftrongly inculcated that [2] *Chrift
came in the flefh.* [3] *God was manifefted in the
flefh.* [4] *The Word was made flefh.* [5] *Chrift
fuffered in the flefh.* [6] *Chrift put to death in
the flefh.* [7] *In him* (Chrift) *dwelleth all the
fulnefs of the Godhead bodily.*

There was reafon for fuch precaution,
and this particular mode of fpeaking. For
herefies arofe in the church very early; and
St. Paul in his own time feems to allude to
apoftacies of this fort, when he fpeaks of
a falling

---

[1] We muft except the words of St. Stephen—*I fee
the fon of man ftanding on the right hand of God.* Acts
vii. 56.

[2] 1 John iv. 2, 3. & v. 6. 2 John 7. [3] 1 Tim. iii. 16.
[4] John i. 14. [5] 1 Pet. iv. 1. [6] 1 Pet. iii. 18. [7] Colof. ii. 9.

[1] *a falling off,* and many errors likely to take place, or already prevalent in the church. And of thefe herefies one was the denying of the humanity of Chrift, and in confequence of it, the refurrection of his body, which is taken notice of by the Apoftle [2] above.

OF THE FIRST, WHO DEPARTED FROM THE DOCTRINE OF THE CHURCH.

One of the firft of thofe, who thus feceded from the Gofpel truth, was Nicolaus; whofe followers received from him the name of Nicolaitæ, and were afterwards incorporated in the multifarious body of the Gnoftics. He was contemporary with the Apoftles, and is mentioned as an apoftate by Saint [3] John. He led the way to this falfe doctrine by faying, that Chrift did not fuffer, nor ever

appear

---

[1] 2 Theff. ii. 3.—1 Tim. iv. 1. [2] 1 Cor. xv. 12, 13.

[3] Rev. ii. 6. and 15. The doctrine of the Nicolaians—*which thing I hate.*

appear in the flesh.—[1] Qui Chriftum ne-
garent in carne veniffe. Another perfon,
Menander, a difciple of Simon Magus, together with Saturninus, infifted, that Chrift
was not gifted with any human fubftance;
and though he might feem to fuffer upon
the crofs; yet he never fuffered, at leaft only
in appearance. In confequence of this, he
denyed any final refurrection.—[2] Chriftum
in fubftantia corporis non fuiffe: et phan-
tafmate tantum quafi paffum fuiffe. Re-
furrectionem carnis nullo modo futuram.
Thefe were followed by [3] Bafilides: who like
them affirmed that the appearance of Chrift
was ideal, and that he was a mere phantafm:
confequently that he had no human frame;

nor

---

[1] Tertullian de Præfcript. Hæreticorum, p. 214. B.
—Chriftum impaffibilem. Irenæus, L. iii. C. xi. p. 218.

[2] Tertullian, p. 219.

[3] — Χριϛυ ως δοκησει πεφηνοτος — ειναι δε φησιν αυτον φαν-
ταϲιαν εν τω φαινεϲθαι, μη ειναι ανθρωπον, μηδε ϲαρκα ειληφεναι.—
υχι Ιηϲυν πεπονθεναι. Epiphanius, V. 1. L. 1. p. 70. See
Irenæus, L. 1. C. 23 p. 98.—alii putative eum paffum.
Ibid. L. 3. C. 17. p. 238.

nor did he ever fuffer. According to him, Simon, the fame who bore the crofs of Chrift, was fubftituted in his room, and fuffered for him.—[1]vice ipfius Simonem crucifixum effe. The Valentinians of the fecond century entertained the like notions about our Saviour. They maintained, that [2] Chrift received nothing from the Virgin Mary: that his body was a heavenly fubftance, which he brought with him from above. This was likewife the opinion of the heretics ftiled Marcionites. Chriftum non veram, fed [3] φανταστικην folum carnem induiffe; nec revera paffum effe, cum pati vifus fuerit. Hence they would not allow, that he was born of the Virgin. In this they agreed with the Gnoftics. For the doctrine, which they fupported, was, that

Chrift

---

[1] Tertull. p. 219. Epiph. L. 1. p. 74.   Irenæus, L. 1. C. xxiii. p. 98.

[2] — μηδιν απο της παρθινικης μητρας ιιληφιναι. αλλα ανωθιν το σωμα ιχιιι. Epiphan. Vol. 1. L. 1. p. 171.

[3] Cave's Hift. Lit. p. 35.

[1] Chrift had no communication with the Virgin, his reputed mother; and never took upon him a human body. Cerdo of the fame age held the like opinion: that [2] Chrift never appeared in the flefh, nor was he the fon of the Virgin; and that he fhewed himfelf under a mere ideal appearance, without any thing [3] real.

Tertullian accordingly fays, that by the fubtilty of their difquifitions they formed fuch devices about the body of Chrift, that they made it either none at all, or any thing but a [4] human body. To obviate thefe

ftrange

---

[1] —Μη ειναι αυτον απο Μαριας γεγεννημενον,——σαρκα δε αυτο, μη ειληφεναι. Epiphanius, L. 1. p. 91.

[2] — Μη ειναι δε τον Χριςον γεγεννημενον εκ Μαριας, μηδε εν σαρκι πεφηνεναι, αλλα δοκησει οντα, και δοκησει πεφηνοτα. Ibid p. 300. Ουδε γαρ ὁ Λογος κατ᾽ αυτες σαρξ γεγονε. Irenæus, L. 1. C. 1. p. 42.

[3] Chriftus φαντασμα. Marcion apud Tertull. L. 3. p. 401. p. 460. Non verbum caro factum eft. Irenæus, L. 1. C. 1. p. 42.

[4] Chrifti carnem quæftionibus diftrahunt, tanquam aut nullam omnino, aut quoquo modo aliam præter humanam. p. 307.

ftrange notions this learned Father wrote his treatife de [1] Refurrectione Carnis; and another differtation de [2] Carne Chrifti, in which he oppofed thofe four principal here-ticks of the fecond century, Bafilides, Mar-cion, Valentinus and Apelles: who denyed that Chrift was in any degree a man.

COROLLARY.

It may feem extraordinary, that fuch an opinion fhould have taken place fo very early: yet that it did take place is moft cer-tain. The reafon for it's thus prevailing may, I think, be eafily difcovered. It arofe from a caufe, which though contrary to the evidence of the Gofpel, and calculated rather to injure the truth, than to promote it, yet indirectly, and ultimately tended to do ho-nour to the divine character of our Saviour. For it arofe from an high opinion of his virtues, and excellence; and a firm belief

of

[1] Page 325.   [2] Page 307.

of the miracles, which he performed; and which in thofe early days, and long after, were never controverted. Thefe virtues, and thefe works, were fo amazing, and fo much beyond what could be expected from mere man, that they would not allow, there was any thing human either in the character or the operations. Hence they admitted the truth; but referred the whole to Chrift as God, without allowing his humanity. For they could not conceive, that any fuch fublime and heavenly qualities, and fuch fupernatural powers, could be the portion of any fon of Adam. Thus they erred, through a mifconception of the true nature of Chrift. They acted however more excufably than many in the days of our Saviour, and in the fucceeding times, who attributed his miracles either to magick, or to the Powers of darknefs. We find, that both acknowledged thefe wonderful works; and faw, and were affured, that no mortal unaffifted could perform them. But they erred in the extreme: the one by denying the intervention of the Deity, the other the operation of man. Yet

we

we find each co-operating obliquely toward the maintenance of thefe evangelical truths, which, however misjudged and mifapplied, were in thofe days acknowledged by the worft enemies of the Gofpel. The fuper-natural powers of Chrift were allowed, though his humanity was fometimes denyed; the allowing of which truth was an article of great confequence.

OF CHRIST PERFECT MAN.

Hence we find a juft reafon for the Apoftles dwelling fo ftrongly upon this ar-ticle, that Chrift *came in the flefh*; and that he *fuffered in the flefh*: and this reafon is particularly given by Saint John, — ότι πολλοι πλανοι εισηλθον εις τον κοσμον, οι μη ομολογχντες Ιησχν Χριςον ερχομενον εν σαρκι. *For many deceivers are entered into the world, who confefs not that Jefus Chrift is come in the flefh.*[1] And he brings this knowledge and this

' 2 John v. 7.

this confeffion, as one teft of Chriftianity. *Hereby know ye, the Spirit of God. Every fpirit, that confeffeth, that Jefus Chrift is come in the flefh, is of God. And every fpirit, that confeffeth not, that Jefus Chrift is come in the flefh, is not of God: and this is that fpirit of Antichrift, whereof ye have heard, that it fhould come; and even now already it is in the world.*[1]

This truth, we find, was of fuch confequence, and thefe herefies fo dangerous, that Saint John, who lived to fee their commencement and increafe, took this particular care to warn his difciples of the mifchief. He therefore in another place brings pofitive proof from his own knowledge, and experience; and infifts, that the Son of God was perfect man. — This he fhews in the following words.—*That, which was from the beginning, which we have heard, which we have feen with our eyes, which we have looked upon* (or contemplated) *and our hands have handled of the* (Logos) *Word of life. For the life*

(that

---

[1] 1 John iv. 2, 3.

(that is the Lord of life), *was manifested, and we have seen it, and bear witness, and shew unto you eternal life, which was with the Father, and was manifested unto us. That which we have seen, and heard, declare we unto you*[1]. We may therefore safely subscribe to the words of Saint Paul, when he tells us — *without controversy great is the mystery of godliness. God was manifest in the flesh; justified in the spirit; seen of angels; preached unto the Gentiles; believed in the world; received up into glory.*[2]

OF PHILO JUDEUS OF ALEXANDRIA.

To these disciples of Basilides and the Gnostics may be joined one of a more serious, and philosophical turn, and of a far superior character, Philo of Alexandria, a Platonick philosopher. He was a Jew by race, and highly respected by those of his

own

[1] 1 John i. 1.   [2] 1 Tim. iii. 16.

own [1] nation, and community. Upon this account he was fent ambaffador to Rome upon a fpecial occafion in the fourth year of the emperour Caligula. This was in the year of Chrift 42: fo that if we fuppofe Philo at this time to have been about forty years of age, he muft have been contemporary with our Saviour all through his life; and nearly of the fame age as many of his Apoftles and Difciples. If he were older, than I have ftated, as fome think, ftill he muft have been throughout contemporary with Chrift; for he furvived him, and, as there is reafon to believe, lived after him many years. We have indeed a confirmation of it from his own words, as will be fhewn hereafter.

He fpeaks at large in many places of the Word of God, the fecond Perfon; which he mentions, as ($\delta \epsilon \nu \tau \epsilon \rho o \varsigma \ \Theta \epsilon o \varsigma$) *the fecond* Divinity, the *great Caufe* of all things, and ftyles him

as

---

[1] $Ta \ \varpi a \nu \tau a \ \iota \nu \delta o \xi o \varsigma$.— $\upsilon \psi \eta \lambda o \varsigma, \ \varkappa a \iota \ \mu \epsilon \tau a \omega \rho o \varsigma$.—
See Jofephus Ant. L. 18. c. 10.

as Plato, as well as the Jews, had done before, the Logos. His thoughts upon this
fubject are very juft and fublime: fuch as
would do honour to a Chriftian. But
though the Jews in his time expected the
Meffiah Prince, and flattered themfelves,
that he would arife among their brethren,
and exalt their nation: yet he fuppreffes
every thought to this purpofe; and intimates
plainly, that, in his opinion, nothing human
or corporal could be annexed to the Son of
God. This prejudice was the great obftacle
to his becoming a Chriftian: though he
muft have been convinced of the miracles
of our Saviour; alfo of the fanctity of his
manners, as well as of his goodnefs and
wifdom. He muft likewife have known
many of the firft profelytes, which were very
numerous at Alexandria; and probably was
not unacquainted with fome of the Apoftles.
But notwithftanding thefe advantages, he
could not bring himfelf to believe, that *the
Word could be made flefh:* and a fuffering
Meffiah, and Chrift crucified, was paft his
comprehenfion. As to the operations of

s

our

our Saviour upon earth, they were too notorious to be denyed. He therefore fays nothing in oppofition: but paffes over the whole in myfterious filence. Hence not a word is to be found in him about Chrift Jefus the Meffiah, nor of his mighty operations: which is extraordinary.

But of the divine Logos, or Word, he fpeaks in many places: and maintains at large the divinity of the fecond Perfon, and defcribes his attributes in a very precife and copious manner, ftyling him,—[1] *τον δευτερον Θεον, ός ες-ιν εκεινε (Θεε πρωτε) Λογος, the fecond Deity, who is the Word of the fupreme God.* [2] *Πρωτογονον υιον, his firft-begotten Son.* [3] *Εικων Θεε. The Image of God:* and [4] *Ποιμην της ιερας αγελης. The Shepherd of his holy flock.*

In his Treatife upon Creation, he fpeaks of the Word, as [5] *the Divine Operator, by whom*

[1] Philo. Fragm. V. ii. p. 625. [2] De Agricult. V. i. p. 308. [3] De Mundi Opif. V. i. p. 6. [4] De Agricult. V. i. p. 308. [5] De Mundi Opif. V. i. p. 4.

whom all things were difposed: and mentions
him as [1] *fuperior to the Angels, and all created beings, and the image and likenefs of God;*
and fays, that *this Image of the true God was
efteemed the fame as God* — [2] ὡς αυτον (Θεον)
κατανοεσι. [3] *This Logos, the Word of God, is
fuperiour to all the world, and more ancient;
being the Productor of all that was produced.*
[4] *The eternal Word of the everlafting God is
the fure and fixed foundation, upon which all
things depend.* He mentions man, as in need
of redemption, and fays,—What intelligent
perfon, who views mankind engaged in un-
worthy and wicked purfuits, but [5] *muft be
grieved to the heart, and call upon that only
Saviour God, that thefe crimes may be exte-
nuated, and that, by a ranfom, and price of
redemption being given for his foul, it may
again obtain it's freedom.* It pleafed God
therefore to appoint his Logos to be a
Medi-

---

[1] De Profugis, V. i. p. 561. [2] De Somniis, V. i.
p. 656. [3] De Leg. Alleg. V. i. p. 121.
[4] De Plantatione Noe, V. i. p. 331. [5] De Confuf.
Ling. V. i. p. 418. l. 50.

Mediator. [1] *To his Word, the chief and most ancient of all in Heaven, the Great Author of the world gave this especial gift, that he should stand as a medium (or* intercessor) *between the Creator and the created. And he is accordingly the Advocate for all mortals. The same* [2] *Word is the Intercessor for man, who is always tending to* [3] *corruption: and he is the appointed Messenger of God, the Governour of all things, to man in subjection to him.* [4] *He therefore exhorts every person, who is able to exert himself in the race, which he is to run, to bend his course without* [5] *remission to the divine Word above,*

[1] Quis Rerum Divin. Hæres. V. i. p. 501, 502.

[2] Ibid. p. 501. l. 49.

[3] For κηραινοντος αει προς το αφθαρτον, we should certainly read προς το φθαρτον.

[4] De Profugis. V. i. p. 560. l. 31.

[5] The present reading is απλιυσι, the meaning of which I do not comprehend. The true reading is probably απνυσι, from απνυσος — *without remission,* — *indesinenter, without stopping to take breath.*

above, who is the Fountain of all wisdom: that by drinking at this sacred Spring, he, instead of death, may obtain the reward of everlasting life.

He repeats continually, that the Logos is the express image of God. [1] *The Word, by which the world was made, is the Image of the supreme Deity.* [2] *As we perceive the sun's light, though the sun is not itself seen; and behold the brightness of the moon, though it's orb may not appear to the eye; so men look up to, and acknowledge, the likeness of God in his minister the Logos, whom they esteem as God.* He attempts to describe his nature by representing him, as [3] *not uncreated, like God; nor yet created, as man:* but of a divine substance.

---

[1] De Monarchiâ, V. ii. L. ii. p. 225. Τον δι αορατον και νοητον Θειον Λογον εικονα λεγει Θευ. De Mundi Opif. V. i. p. 6.

[2] De Somniis. V. i. p. 656. l. 33.

[3] Quis Rer. Divin. Hæres. V. i. p. 502.

ſubſtance. [1] *For the Word of God, which is above all the hoſt of Heaven, cannot be comprehended by human viſion, having nothing in his nature, that is perceptible to mortal ſenſe. For being the Image of God, and the eldeſt of all intelligent beings, he is ſeated immediately next to the One God, without any interval of ſeparation.* This in the language of Scriptures is — *ſitting on the right hand of God.* He adds — [2] *For not being liable to any voluntary or involuntary change, or falling off, he has God for his lot, and portion, and his reſidence is in God.* The like is mentioned in another place, where he is repreſented again as ſinleſs, and as the great High Prieſt of the world. [3] *We maintain, that by the* (true) *High Prieſt is not meant a man; but the divine Word; who is free from all voluntary, and involuntary tranſgreſſions — being of heavenly*

[1] De Profugis. V. i. p. 561. l. 16.

[2] Ibid. l. 24.

[3] Ibid. p. 562. l. 13.

venly parentage; *born of God, and of that divine Wifdom, by which all things were produced.* He fpeaks to the fame purpofe in another place, where he makes mention of the word — [1] εν ᾦ και Αρχιερευς, ὁ πρωτογονος αυτα (Θεα) Θειος Λογος —*In which prefides that High Prieft, the Holy Word, the firft-born of God;* — at other times ftyled πρεσβυτατος υιος Θεα. — *The Son of God, antecedent to all creation.* [2] Τατον μεν γαρ πρεσβυτατον υιον ὁ των οντων ανετειλε Πατηρ, ὁν ετερωθι πρωτογονον ωνομασε. It is manifeft, that every article, which the Sacred Writers have given to Chrift in his mediatorial capacity, Philo has attributed to him in his divine character antecedent to creation.

[1] De Somniis, Vol. i. p. 653.

[2] De Confuf. Ling. V. i. p. 414.

OF THE OPINION OF PHILO CONCERNING THE LOGOS BEING REPRESENTED AS HIGH PRIEST.

Such was the opinion of Philo Judeus in respect to the Logos, or Word of God; whose divine nature he maintains, and his origination from God, Yet, though the Scriptures had declared, that this High Prieſt was the Meſſiah appointed to come into the world, and our Saviour by his doctrine and miracles had proved himſelf to be that Meſſiah, Philo by his ſilence ſhews, that he could not accede to that opinion. He could not admit of a crucified Saviour. It was a ſtumbling block in the way of truth, by which he was continually impeded. When therefore he comes to his fourth queſtion de Profugis, (p. 561) where it is ſaid from [1] Numbers xxxv. 25 — 28, that the guilty perſon, who fled for his crimes to a city of refuge, ſhould remain there *to*

the

[1] Alſo Joſhua xx. 6.

*the death of the High Priest, who was anointed
with the holy oil;* he owns, that this embarraffed him greatly.—[1] Ἡ προθεσμια — τυ Αρχιερεως ὁ θανατος, πολλην εν τω ῥητω μοι παρεχυσα
δυσκολιαν. *This article, concerning the death of
the High Priest, has, from the words, in which it
is signified, afforded me much difficulty and trouble.*
He perceived, that this was typical, and that
the Logos, or Word, whom he acknowledges
to be the great High Prieſt, was ultimately
ſignified. And though he refines greatly, and
miſapplies the intelligence afforded him, yet
he owns, that by the death of the High Prieſt
ſpiritual vaſſalage and exile were to ceaſe,
and the guilty perſon was to be ſet free, and
return to the ſtate, which he had forfeited.[2]
Theſe truths he certainly ſaw ; but could
not conceive in what manner it was poſſible
for the Logos, or great High Prieſt, to
die. He did not conſider, that, as the Word
had appeared, as he intimates, (κατ᾽ εικονα
ανθρωπος) in a human form to the Patriarchs,

he

---

[1] De Profugis, V. i. p. 561. l. 48.

[2] ib. 513 l. 27. p. 534 l. 44.

he might again fubmit to the fame form,
and as a man fuffer death. This he could
not conceive. It was a prejudice too ftrong
to be removed. He had undoubtedly converfed with Chriftians at ' Alexandria; alfo
at Rome, when he went to that city at two
different intervals. He was probably con-
verfant with them likewife at Jerufalem.
For this feems to have been the place of his
refidence in the early part of his life. He
ftyles it, ιερα πολις, and fays,—Αυτη, καθαπερ
εφην, εμη μεν εςι πατρις, Μητροπολις δε ὁ μιας
χωρας Ιεδαιας, αλλα και των πλειςων.[2] *This
city* (Jerufalem) *was the place of my birth:
which city is the metropolis not of Judea only,
but of many other regions.* And this city he
feems to have vifited at the times of the
Paffover in obedience to the law: and probably at other feafts.[3] From his intercourfe
with

---

[1] The Chriftians were very early fo numerous at
Alexandria, that it was thought neceffary to have a
church founded, and a bifhop appointed.

[2] De Virtut. V. ii. p. 587.

[3] See Philo Frag. Vol. ii. p. 646.

with the Chriftians, he obtained this improved knowledge concerning the Word of
God, whom he ftyles the Son of God, his
firft-begotten: whofe divine nature he has
defcribed more truly by far, than any of the
Platonifts before him; or any of the Alex-
andrine fchool after him; or even than any
of his own nation of old. But Chrift crucified feems to have been fo contrary to his
pre-conceived notions, that he never mentions him, nor alludes to him, though he
lived in his time, and muft have been well
acquainted with the hiftory of his holy life,
and doctrines, and all his wonderful works.
And there is fomething extraordinary in his
filence, which is worth obferving. For as
he had fo very often taken pains to declare,
what the Word of God was; we fhould
naturally expect, that he would likewife
have fhewn, what it was not. And as our
Saviour gave out to all, that he was the Son
of God, the firft-born of the world, who
came down from heaven to give his life a
ranfom for many; and was pointed out by
Saint Paul as the High Prieft mentioned by
the

the Prophets; it is extraordinary, that he
does not try to obviate this notion. The
fame and the pretenfions of Chrift, the
Meffiah, were well known among the Jews
in the time of Philo. They could be no
fecret at Alexandria, which was the refidence
of fome thoufands of his nation; and which
was fo near to Judea: efpecially as Saint
Mark preached the Gofpel there very early;
and as is generally fuppofed A. C. 49. Yet
he never attempts to fet afide thefe pretenfions; nor does he ever fpeak of Chrift, or
of Jefus, the Meffiah. His prejudices
would not fuffer him to acknowledge Chrift
in the flefh : and at the fame he muft have
been affected by his holy life and miracles :
for *thefe things were not done in a corner.*
He had certainly canvaffed this article in
his own mind, and was brought over fo far
towards the truth, that he confeffed, it was
more eafy to conceive a Deity partaking of
the human nature, than a man partaking
of divinity —[1] Θαττον γαρ αν εις ανθρωπον Θεον,

η εις

---

[1] De Virtut. V. ii. p. 562.

η εις Θεον ανθρωπον μεταβαλειν. He was, as he confeffes, under great doubts and difficulties: and, as he could not accede, he kept an awful diftance; maintaining a religious filence: and what he could not be brought through frailty to admit, he was neither able nor willing to deny. He feems to have ftood in a fearful medium; which was the cafe of Jofephus and of many of the Jews at that feafon.

From the extracts produced above, we may learn, what was the opinion of Philo, and others of his nation, concerning the divinity of the fecond Perfon, the Logos, or Word of God. And in him we find the doctrine more improved, and more precifely given, than it was ever afforded, before the coming of Chrift.

Though I have introduced this learned Writer with Bafilides and the Gnoftics, and others of the firft and fecond century; yet he differs from them in one refpect greatly. They agree with him in not allowing, that

Chrift

Chrift came in the flefh: but they grant,
that he did come in a fpiritual manner, and
that Chrift, the Meffiah, was that Perfon.
But Philo fays nothing of his appearing
upon earth, and feems tacitly to deny it,
dwelling only upon the prior and heavenly
character of the Logos, or Word; and de-
fcribing his divine nature, by fhewing that
he was the Son of God, and firft-born of the
world. Yet he feems fometimes to verge
towards the truth, when in mentioning the
different characters of the πρωτογονος Λογος,
the firft-begotten Word, he reprefents him, [1] ὁ
κατ᾽ εικονα ανθρωπος, *in the likenefs of man.*

He is faid by different writers to have
converfed with the firft Chriftians; and to
have got much intelligence from them.
We find it mentioned by [2] Eufebius, that at
Rome he had accefs to Saint Peter; and the
fame is faid by [3] Jerome. Thus much is certain,

[1] De Confuf. Ling. Vol. i. p. 427.

[2] Eufeb. Hift. Ecclef. L. ii. C. xvii. V. i. p. 65.

[3] S. Hieron. de Script. Ecclef. Vol. iv. p. 106.

tain, that he has borrowed the fentiments and doctrines of the Apoftles, and firft Chriftians: in confequence of which he muft have had fome intercourfe, and cor-refpondence with them.

CONCERNING THE AGE OF PHILO.

As I have fuppofed, that fuch excellent knowledge could not have been obtained by this early Jew, but by his accefs to fome of the early Chriftians, it will be proper to fhew, that the æra of his life correfponds with the firft promulgation of the Gofpel. This is denyed by the learned editor of his Works,[1] who maintains that he was born many years before Chrift, and could not have had any correfpondence with Saint Mark, and the firft Chriftians of Alexandria. The reafons, which he gives, I fhall now examine.

He

[1] Dr. Mangey.

He tells us, that many have undertaken
to ſtate the time of Philo's birth: concerning
which however we have no determinate
intelligence. Some, he ſays, who ſeem to
come neareſt to the truth, make it to have
been about thirty years before the birth of
our Saviour. This was the opinion of
Baſnage: and the Editor of Philo agrees
with him; and gives the following reaſon
for his determination —[1] Ille enim ipſe anno
Caii quarto, urbis conditæ 793, ſe ſenem et
ætate provectiorem plus una vice teſtatur.
This is a great miſtake, into which I wonder, how the Editor could poſſibly lapſe.
Philo at the beginning of his [2] Treatiſe,
where an account is given of his embaſſy,
undoubtedly ſpeaks of himſelf, as old. But
by this he meant, at the time of his writing,
not at the time of the embaſſy to Caligula,
which was probably twenty years, or more,
antecedent. This is manifeſt to any body,
who will examine the Treatiſe: and I wonder,

[1] Præfatio, p. ii.

[2] De Virtutibus, V. ii. 545.

der, how it could be miſtaken. We find in
the account given a moſt ſevere invective
againſt the emperour; ſuch as no Jew, nor
any perſon of whatever country, would have
dared to have uttered. The Jewiſh nation
had been in great dread of Caligula: who
had threatened to introduce his ſtatue into
the temple at Jeruſalem. Upon their repeated remonſtrances he became hoſtile to
the whole nation; and ſhewed a particular
diſaffection towards the Jews of Alexandria;
which place he purpoſed to viſit. To avert
his anger, it was thought proper to ſend an
embaſſy to Rome: and Philo with ſome
others was employed for this purpoſe; and
he ſaw the emperour at Rome and at
Puteoli: but he met with nothing favourable. On the contrary, he was ' inſulted,
put in chains, and hardly eſcaped with his
life. In conſequence of this, he ſome years
afterwards wrote the Treatiſe De ² Legatiōne:

in

' Philo, V. ii. p. 597, 545.

² Styled alſo, Πιρι Αριτων, or De Virtutibus, ſive De
Legatione.

in which he accuſes Caligula of [1] folly, madneſs, cruelty, and every vice. This he is ſuppoſed by his Editor to have produced in the very year of his embaſſy; at the very criſis, when the Jewiſh nation was under ſuch apprehenſions. But this could not have been the caſe. No perſon would have publiſhed ſuch a ſatire in the reign of Caligula, nor for ſome time after. Hence nothing concerning the age of Philo can be collected from theſe data.

Euſebius however mentions a tradition, that Philo read this Treatiſe before the emperour Claudius, and the whole ſenate; and that it was received with great applauſe.[2] This is undoubtedly a Jewiſh figment. The author upon ſuch an occaſion would have introduced ſome compliments to the reigning prince, as well as to the aſſembly, before whom he ſtood. But

[1] —μυρια περι την αρχην (τȣ Γαΐȣ) ενυβρισαντος.
Euſeb. Hiſt. Eccleſ. L. ii. C. v. V. i. p. 51.

[2] Euſeb. Hiſt. Eccleſ. L. ii. C. xviii. V. i. p. 72.

But not a word to this purpofe occurs; nor
are they ever mentioned. Befides, he fpeaks
of the Romans in general with much bit-
ternefs; and accufes them of cruelty, and
illiberality, towards him and his people.
How can we fuppofe, that fuch an invective
could have been permitted by the fenate;
or that they would at any rate have liftened
either to fatire or to encomium from a Jew?
But what puts the matter out of all doubt,
he himfelf fhews, that it could not be written even in the time of Claudius, much lefs
in the time of Caligula: for he intimates
repeatedly in the courfe of his work, that
the former prince, Claudius, had been for
fome time dead. One of the chief enemies
of the Jews was an Egyptian, named Helicon: who had employed every art to make
them odious to the emperour. ¹ *But this
Helicon*, fays Philo, *was at laft taken off;
being put to death by Claudius Cæfar for fome
other*

¹ Ὁ δὶ Ἑλικὼν ὑπο Κλαυδια Γιρμανικα Καισαρος αναιρεθιις, ιφ'
δις αλλοις ὁ φιλοβλαβης ηδικησιν· αλλα ταυτα μιν ὑστερον ιγινιτο.
De Virt. five de Legatione, V ii. p. 576.

other base actions, of which he had been guilty. But these things happened afterwards: that is, after my embassy to Rome. This is in the very Treatise de Legatione. He here intimates plainly, that the reign of Claudius was past, when he wrote this document: and Caligula consequently must have been for some years dead. The like is to be found in his oration against Flaccus.[1] But why do I mention this oration? when in the very treatise above-mentioned,[2] with which we are concerned, it appears throughout, almost from every page, that Caligula was then dead: the whole character given is of a person departed. We must not therefore take for granted, that an event, and the history of an event, are necessarily of the same date. The one may have been many years after the other. The Treatise therefore could not have been written till the reign of Nero: and probably later; when the Cæsarean family was extinct; and no offence could be

given

[1] Philo. Vol. ii. p. 517.

[2] De Virtut. sive de Legatione.

C 2

given by the publication. For had it been made known at the time fuppofed, Apion, his great enemy, would foon have accufed him to the præfect of Egypt: and he would have forfeited his life in a few hours.

It may feem unneceffary after thefe proofs to mention any more of the arguments, which the Editor has introduced in fupport of his opinion. But as there is one, upon which he feems to lay great ftrefs, I will not pafs it unnoticed. [1] Philo incidently mentions the fate of the Xanthians in Lycia; who were all deftroyed by the army of Brutus A. U. C. 712, for their attachment to Cæfar. The hiftory is introduced in the following manner—Ὡσπερ φασιν, ε προ πολλε, κ τ. λ. *As they fay, not long ago,* &c. Hence he fuppofes, that the Author fpeaks of the affair as a recent event — ut facto recenti, loquitur.[2] But by the words *not long ago*

---

[1] Vol. ii. p. 464. The event is alfo mentioned by Dion Caffius, L. xlvii. C. xxxiv. V. i. p. 514.

[2] Præf. ad Philonis Op. p. ii.

ago, and *not long fince*, is fignified a very unlimited fpace of time; which can only be
determined by the Author: for it depends
intirely upon his mode of judging, and the
termini, to which he tacitly alludes. If a
perfon were writing upon migiations and
difcoveries, he might fay, that it is not long
fince, that America was difcovered. Yet it
has been known for above three centuries.
Nothing therefore can be precifely gathered
from the words above: nor can the year of
a man's life be determined by fuch evidence.
The very words — Ὥσπερ φασιν, *as they fay*,
feem to intimate much uncertainty, and
that the fact was by no means recent. In
fhort, we may prove it from the Author's
own account of himfelf, and his writings;
before which all fuch furmifes muft va-
nifh.

When therefore the birth of Philo is carried up to the time of Julius Cæfar, it is an
unwarrantable anticipation. There is reafon
to think, that he was nearly of the fame age
as the Apoftles; with fome of whom he is faid

to

to have converfed. He was alive, we have feen, fo late as the reign of Nero. And as he refided at Alexandria, he could not fail of knowing Saint Mark, who was the firft bifhop in that place,[1] and came thither (as the Editor allows[2]) about the year 48, or 49. And, if St. Mark's Gofpel was publifhed in that year, or, as many think, before that year, then Philo had an opportunity of feeing it alfo. Moreover, fince he was living, when Nero was emperour, it is not impro-bable, that he had converfed with fome of the difciples of Chrift, as well as of the Apoftles, and that he was not a ftranger to the writings of fome of the other Evangelifts. His fituation and time of life will warrant this conjecture, and, above all, the truths, which he has difclofed.

THIS

---

[1] Τϑτον δὲ Μαρκον πρωτον φασιν επι της Αιγυπτϑ ϛειλαμενον, το Ειαγγελιον, ὁ δη και ϛιεγραψατο, κηρυξαι, Εκκλησιας τι πρωτον επ' αυτης Αλιξαιδειας ϛιϛησαϛθαι. Eufeb. Hift. Ecclef. L. ii. C. xvi. V. i. p. 65.

[2] Novennio poft Caii obitum, fcil. anno Chrifti 49, Marcus Alexandriam venit. Præfat. ad Philonis Opera,

THIS ARGUMENT CONTROVERTED.

The Editor is of a different opinion; which he expreſſes in the following manner. Verum meɪito dubitatur, anne quivis Fœderis Novi liber, dum Philo per ætatem poſſet ſcribere, editus fuerit in lucem. Certe nulla ex Epiſtolis Paulinis, et quod ad D. Marci Evangelium attinet, Euſebius ejus promulgationem refert ad annum Claudii Cæſaris tertium . . . . verum ſi Irenæo fides, iſque antiquior et potior Euſebio teſtis, non editum eſt Evangelium iſtud, niſi poſt obitum Petri et Pauli, id eſt anno Æræ Chriſtianæ 64, quando Philo prope centenarius fuerat.[1] Though this date (A. C. 64) be allowed in reſpeċt to the promulgation of the Goſpel; yet all that I have maintained may be ſtill true. For at this period (A.C. 64), Philo, ſo far from being near an hundred years old, was probably not older than many of the Apoſtles. If we ſuppoſe him to have been forty, or forty two years old,

when

[1] Præf. ad Philonis Op. p. iii.

c 4

when he was fent to Rome, he was but
fixty four, when Saint Peter and Saint Paul
fuffered martyrdom. He might therefore
very eafily have had, if not an intimacy,
yet an acquaintance, with them and their
difciples, and have read their Epiftles.

But the chief proof, that he had perufed
fome of the Books of the New Teftament,
or at leaft had converfed with fome of
the firft converts to Chriftianity, is to
be drawn from his writings: in which, as
I have fhewn, are many articles of great
confequence to be found. A perfon,
who fpeaks of the Word of God, as the
Son of God, his *Firft-begotten*, the *Shepherd
of his flock*, the *fecond Great Caufe*, the *Image
of God*, the *Mediator between God and man*,
the *Great High Prieft* mentioned by the Prophets, the *Creator of all, that was created*;
who fpeaks alfo of *Redemption*, and — λυτρα
και σωςρα — the *Price of Redemption*, and of
the Perfon, by whom it was to be procured,
and by whom we are finally to attain to
(ζωην αιδιον) *everlafting life:* I fay, who-
e̶ ines,
                                        ould

could be no ſtranger to Chriſt and Chriſtianity. Euſebius therefore very juſtly obſerves,
that Philo muſt have had in idea ſome of
the firſt preachers of the Goſpel, and the
doctrines tranſmitted by the Apoſtles themſelves, when he wrote theſe things. But
this is not ſufficiently precife : for he had
not theſe truths tranſmitted. He lived in
the time of the Evangeliſts and Apoſtles;
and obtained his knowledge from them, the
fountain head. And that' he entertained a
favourable opinion of the Goſpel, we may
judge from his ſilence: for though a Jew,
and, as one in conſequence of it would ſuppoſe, not a friend to Chriſtianity; yet, when
there are many opportunities afforded, he
never ſpeaks againſt it. And we have ſeen,
that he borrows many eſſential truths, which
could not have been obtained from any un-
converted people of his own nation. At
the ſame time it is to be obſerved, that
though he lived among Chriſtians, and was
acquainted with their doctrines, yet he never
mentions them; nor does he ever take notice
of Saint Mark, who preſided in his time
over the church at Alexandria.

Yet

Yet so much was Philo beholden to them, that we may read in him the opinion of the Apostles, and the doctrines of Christ himself, about this essential article of our belief. And that he had opportunities of information is plain. For if he were, as the Editor thinks, antecedent to Christ in respect to his birth, it is very manifest from his own evidence, that he survived him: for in his Treatise, about which we are concerned, he mentions, as I have shewn, the death of Claudius. He was therefore alive through the whole course of our Saviour's residence upon earth; and survived him several years. This shews, what room there was for intelligence; of which, it is plain, he availed himself. He was a Jew, and a follower of Plato. But what he says of the first-born Son of God, the Creator of all things, the Image of God, the Mediator, &c. was past the apprehension of man. Neither Plato, nor the Stoicks, had any thing similar; and even the Jews had nothing adequate to the precise truths, which he discloses. He certainly has adopted so much from Christianity,

nity, that Photius fuppofes, that he was a
profelyte, but relapfed. For this however
we have no evidence: on the contrary, Philo
intimates through all his works, that he
continued in the religion of his fathers.

Such is the atteftation of Philo Judeus;
which muft be efteemed of the greateft confequence. For he lived in the time of our
Saviour, and of his Apoftles: and their
doctrines he has manifeftly borrowed. They
are not confined to any particular part of
his works; but are to be found in different
treatifes: and I have produced them in his
own words to the reader; and much more
I might have produced: but thefe, to which
I have applied, feem fufficient. His evidence
is plain: and though he was in general
much given to abftrufe and myftical notions,
yet in thefe inftances he is perfectly precife,
and. clear; and fpeaks without difguife the
opinion of thofe, from whom he got his
information; and affords us fometimes the
language, as well as the fentiments, of the
Apoftles. As he lived fo near to Judea, and

shews

ſhews in his writings, that he was born in
thoſe parts, he may have borrowed ſome of
theſe doctrines from a ſtill higher ſource.
As this, though probable, is not certain,
let us abide by that evidence, which he
gives, whether he obtained his knowledge
from one, or many. That it was borrowed
at the firſt promulgation of the Goſpel, is
manifeſt: and the great truth, which reſults
from it, cannot, I think, be controverted.

THE ACCOUNT OF THE LOGOS, OR WORD OF GOD, IN SAINT JOHN.

We have ſeen, that the Hereticks above-
mentioned would not allow, that Chriſt
came upon earth in a human ſtate: and
Philo by his particular ſilence ſeems to think,
that he did not appear at all. This denyal
of our Saviour in the fleſh I have ſhewn to
have been of a very dangerous conſequence;
and rendered the ſufferings of Chriſt, and
his death, and paſſion, together with all the
bleſſings which were to enſue, abortive and
ineffectual.

ineffectual. Saint John therefore, in whose time these base notions began to spread, took early care to remedy this mischief, and to shew the human, as well as the divine, nature of the Messiah. And as Plato and his disciples, and the Jews likewise, before the time of Philo, used the term Logos to express the [1] *Word of God*; Saint John adopts the

---

[1] The word Λογος in the original is דבר and מלת.— Dober and Malat: which the Helleniſtic Jews very properly tranſlated Λογος, the Verbum of the Romans. It occurs as a Perſon, the Angel of the Covenant, in ſeveral parts of the Greek Verſion. — μιχρι τε ελθειν τον Λογον αυτε, το Λογιον τε Κυριε. Pſalm cv. 19.

Απεςειλε τον Λογον αυτε, και ιασατο αιτες. Pſ. cvii. 20. *He ſent his Word and healed them.*

Εις τον αιωνα ὁ Λογος σε διαμενει εν τω ερανω. Pſ. cxix. 89.

In Wiſdom — Ὁ παντοδιναμος σε Λογος απ᾽ ηρανων εκ θρονων {lege εκδοραν} βασιλειων — εις μεσον της ολεθριας ηλατο γης. C. xviii. 15.

The Patriarch Jacob ſpeaks of the Word under the name of God's Angel.— *The Angel, which redeemed me from all evil.* Gen. xlviii. 16.

The Memra of the Chaldee Paraphraſts.

the fame: and by his fuperiour doctrine tries to remedy their miftakes, and to enforce the truth. This he performs moft clearly, I think, and moft fatisfactorily, in the firft chapter of his Gofpel.

SAINT JOHN'S GOSPEL, CHAP. I.

" 1. In the beginning was the Word, and the Word was with God, and the Word was God.

2. The fame (Word) was in the beginning with God.

3. All things were made by ¹ it (the Word) and

---

¹ Our verfion renders the word αυτε, *him*, and this is the proper meaning. But I have ufed the word *it*; be- caufe feveral have rendered the original in this manner, in order to get rid of a difficulty, which embarraffed them: as they wanted to prove, that by the *Word* was meant *no Perfon*. But fo plain is the text, that tranflate the word either way, ftill a *Perfon* muft be fignified: and the truth cannot be evaded by this artifice.

and without it (without the Word) was not any thing made, that was made.

4. In it (in the Word) was life: and the life was the Light of men.

5. And the Light (of the Word or Logos) ſhineth in darkneſs, and the darkneſs comprehended it not."

The Apoſtle then by an apoſtrophe introduces the perſon, who was the forerunner of Chriſt, and who firſt declared him to the world.

" 6. There was a man ſent from God, whoſe name was John.

7. The ſame came for a witneſs, to bear witneſs of the Light (the Word), that all men through him might believe (in the Word)."

Concerning the Perſon, of whom John bare witneſs, there can be no doubt: and

con-

confequently it is very plain, who is meant above by Life, and Light.

" 8. He (John) was not that Light (the Word), but was fent to bear witnefs of that Light (the Word)."

Had the Word, this Light of the world, never appeared in the flefh, or had the Word been the phantafm of Bafilides, and the Valentinians, this caution about Saint John would have been quite unneceffary. The Baptift could never have been taken for a phantom. It therefore muft be a perfon, a human being here fpoken of, and with whom he is contrafted.

" 9. That (Word) was the true Light, which lighteth every man, that cometh into the world.

10. It (the Word before mentioned; the Light, of which John bare witnefs) was in the world, and the world was made by it (the Word), and the world knew it not:

(knew

(knew not the Logos, the Word of light, and life)."

We have here the two natures of Chrift plainly alluded to. His heavenly character, as Creator, and his humanity are both fpecified. And though I make ufe of the word *it*, which is not properly applicable to a perfon, yet we fhall throughout find, that a perfon is fpoken of.

11. " It (the Word, the Light of the world) came unto it's own; and it's own (in general) received it not..

12. But as many as received it, (the Logos or Word) to them it gave the power to become the fons of God, even to them that believed in it's (the Word's) name."

Who could give this power to become the fons of God, but the Son of God, who was with God, and was God, by whom all things

D   were

were created?—[1] ὁ δευτερος Θεος, ὁς εςιν εκεινε Λογος—*the second Divinity of* Philo, *which is the Word of God* —[2] εικων Θεε, δι᾽ ἑ συμπας ὁ κοσμος εδημιεργειτο— *that Image of God, by whom the whole world was created* — the fame, who forgave fins. It is therefore manifeft, that however the terms ἑτος and αυτος may be rendered by particular perfons, the artifice will avail little; for a Perfon is manifeftly fignified.

All this is furely very plain; and an article, to which every unprejudiced perfon muft accede. But it is faid to be a myftery. True. But what is this myftery, but a divine truth, which we could not have known, but by information? Take away the fanctity of the object, there will be found as much myftery in the freezing of water, when told to a perfon, who never beheld it; or in the properties of the magnet to one, who had never before heard of them. Our faith upon thefe occafions

[1] Philo apud Eufeb. Præp. Evang. L. vii. C. xiii. p. 323.

[2] Id. . . . L. ii. V. ii. p. 225.

occasions depends upon the credibility of the informer. If the intelligence comes from the mouth of truth, we muſt believe it; or we act contrary to reaſon. And there would be no difficulty in this caſe, were it not for the pride, and prejudice of men. Therefore this poſitive and determinate evidence, which cannot be ſet aſide, they try to extenuate, and ſoften; till by refinement they reduce it to nothing. But ſtill there are other myſteries, or elſe the Goſpel muſt be given up. We have an inſtance to this purpoſe afforded us by Saint Matthew, who gives it in the very words of our Saviour. [1] *All things are delivered unto me of my Father: and no man knoweth the Son, but the Father: neither knoweth any man the Father, ſave the Son, and he, to whomſoever the Son will reveal him.* We find, that the myſtery of the Son is like the myſtery of the Father: which myſtery of the Father, however certain we may be of his exiſtence, muſt be eſteemed the greateſt that can be; far beyond our conception. And to the knowledge of theſe

myſteries

[1] Matth. xi. 27.

myſteries no man can of himſelf arrive
Had Chriſt been merely a man upon earth,
there could have been no ſuch myſtery;
conſequently no difficulty in obtaining an
immediate knowledge of him. And he
accordingly, as a man, was known to all
about him. But additionally to this he had
in his nature ſomething heavenly and ſupe-
riour, his Divinity known to the Father
only; therefore not to be diſcovered by man,
who can only know it by divine revelation.

In reſpect to the Divinity of our Saviour,
there is one paſſage in Saint Paul, ſo plain
and determinate, that I ſhould think every
reaſonable perſon muſt neceſſarily give it his
aſſent. The Apoſtle is mentioning his zeal
and beſt wiſhes for ſome of the proſelytes to
the Goſpel, and adds—ʹΙνα παρακληθωσιν αι
καρδιαι αυτων, συμβιβασθεντων εν αγαπη, και εις
παντα πλ8τον της πληροφοριας της συνεσεως, εις
επιγνωσιν τ8 μυ5ηρι8 τ8 Θε8, και Πατρος, και τ8
Χρι58. ʹ *That their hearts might be comforted,
being knit together in love, and unto all riches of*
the

*the full affurance of underftanding, to the ac-
knowledgement of the myftery of God, and of the
Father, and of Chrift.* This latter part is
neither here, nor in the Roman verfion,
properly tranflated. Hence the purport of
the Apoftle's information is in great meafure
ruined. The words — *την επιγνωσιν τ8 μυςηρι8
τ8 Θε8, και Πατρος και τ8 Χρις8*—fhould be rendered — *to the knowledge of the myftery of God,*
BOTH OF THE FATHER AND OF THE SON;
or more fully— BOTH OF GOD THE FATHER,
AND OF GOD THE SON. This is the true
purport of thefe fignificant terms, if there
be any certainty in language: and I fhould
think, that upon due confideration it could
not be controverted. The Divinity of our
Saviour is here clearly afcertained: and his
connexion with God is very juftly called a
myftery: for it was a truth not to be difcovered by man. *Flefh and blood could not
have revealed it.* Chrift in this paffage is
not only mentioned with God, but as God
—that Chrift, *who is over all, God bleffed for
ever.*[1] *Θεος ευλογητος εις τ8ς αιωνας.*

OF

[1] Rom. ix. 5.

OF THE THIRD PERSON.

If the Divinity of our Saviour be satis-
factorily proved, and we are affured of the
fecond Perfon, the Son of God, the third
follows of courfe, and cannot but be admitted. When our Saviour gave his laft
command to his difciples, and ordered them
*to teach all nations, baptizing them in the
name of the Father, and of the Son, and of the
Holy Ghoft,*[1] we cannot fuppofe, that, on fo
folemn an occafion, after mentioning two
Perfons, he would thirdly mention along
with them, and exactly in the fame manner,
a mere mode, or attribute, and that too an
attribute of one of thofe perfons. The facred
Writers could never wifh to perplex the
world, much lefs to miflead thofe, to whom
they addreffed themfelves. And therefore, if
the Holy Spirit did not, as a Perfon, exift,
they would not have made it a co-operating
agent, nor an agent at all. Yet they fpeak
of the Holy Ghoft as the Paraclete, or

Com-

[1] Matth. xxviii. 19.

Comforter; and record it, as faid by Chrift, that to fin againft the Holy Ghoft is an unpardonable fin. It is mentioned, that the Apoftles were [1] prompted, directed, and furthered by the Holy Ghoft: and Saint Paul mentions his being controuled by the Holy Ghoft [2]; and fays, *it feemed good to the Holy Ghoft*. [3] And our very knowledge of Chrift is faid to be by *the Holy Ghoft*. [4] He is continually fpoken of as an Agent, and Perfon: and his influence, gifts, and power, are continually afcertained. [5] It is not to be fuppofed, that the Apoftles would have fpoken fo repeatedly of the Holy Spirit and it's operations, if no fuch operator had exifted. They could as eafily have referred thefe bleffings, and this influence, immediately to the Father, and to the Father alone; had there not been a third

Perfon,

---

[1] 1 Cor. ii. 13. *Which things alfo we fpeak, not in the words, which man's wifdom teacheth, but which the Holy Ghoft teacheth.*

[2] Acts xvi. 6, 7. [3] Acts xv. 28.

[4] 1 Cor. xii. 3. [5] Heb. ii. 4.

Perfon, through whom by the appointment of the Father they were derived. Hence we are ordered not to refift the Holy Spirit; nor to grieve it, nor to fin againft it—That Spirit, *the Comforter, which is the Holy Ghoft,* which was to come after Chrift's death, and *to teach* the Difciples *all things.*[1] Our Saviour accordingly tells his Difciples — [2] *If I go not away, the Comforter will not come: but if I depart, I will fend him unto you.* Had the Holy Spirit been merely the divine influence, and not a Perfon, our Saviour would have expreffed himfelf accordingly; and inftead of *Comforter* would have mentioned *comfort. If I go not,* you will receive no comfort: *but if I depart, I will fend* comfort *unto you.* But he manifeftly fpeaks of a Perfon.[3]

But ftill doubts have prevailed; and it has been thought extraordinary, that, as thefe

[1] John xiv. 26.   [2] John xvi. 7.

[3] The evidences to this purpofe in Scripture are very numerous: but I fhall not apply to them any farther ;

as

thefe articles are of fuch confequence, the facred Writers have not dwelt more fully upon them. To this it may be anfwered, that they are fufficiently explicit, and intelligible to any perfon, who will confider them without prejudice. The Evangelifts ftudied to be brief and contracted. Hence we have from them more matter in a fmall compafs, than from any other writers in the world. If there be any difficulties, they are to be furmounted: and Divine Providence has acted in this inftance, as in many others. We muft dig in the mine to obtain the ore;

we

as they have been already collected, and placed in a proper light by perfons of much judgment and learning. There are alfo fome recent publications upon thefe articles, which cannot but give the reader great fatisfaction. Among thefe are two very excellent Sermons by Dr. Eveleigh, Provoft of Oriel College, Oxford; alfo a Sermon by the Rev. Mr. Veyfie, Fellow of the fame College; and a learned Treatife by the Rev. Mr. Hawtrey, of Bampton, Oxfordfhire. In the writings of thefe learned gentlemen will be found all the material texts of Scripture, which relate to the prefent fubject. The Rev. Dr. Cæfar Morgan alfo has written a Treatife full of erudition upon Philo; which, though he differs from me, deferves to be well confidered.

we muft labour in the field to enjoy the
harveft. A heathen poet has delivered this
great truth in a very expreffive manner.

—— Pater ipfe colendi
Haud facilem effe viam voluit: primufque per artem
Movit agros, curis acuens mortalia corda:
Nec torpere gravi paflus fua regna veterno.

A like labour of the mind, with a fimilar
exeicife of our faculties, is requifite in order
to obtain knowledge, both human and divine. And this is the very purpofe of that
Being, who confers the blefling. We muft
feek, to find; and knock, to have it opened.
From difcoveries hence made, we learn what
a number of latent truths are to be found
in the Scriptures. And when thefe upon
examination are obferved, they afford more
inward fatisfaction, and are more conducive
to faith, than if they were fuperficial and
felf-evident. They likewife increafe our
regard for the Scriptures. For the more we
difcover of latent defign and wifdom in an
object, the greater will be our veneration,
and the ftronger our faith.

From

From the foregoing difquifition, we may with grief perceive, how perverfe and fickle the minds of men are; and what contrariety and inconfiftency appear in their feveral opinions. Many of the principal innovators in the firft age of the church would not believe, that Chrift came in the flefh; and denyed his humanity. In this age it is become a fafhion to deny his divinity: and many, we find, infift, that he was a mere man, with all the frailties of the fons of Adam. Hence his character of the Son of God, and of God, of the Angel of the Covenant, of the Interceffor, Mediator, and Redeemer, are totally fet afide; and his miraculous birth efteemed a fable.

THE EVIDENCE OF SOME OF THE MOST EARLY FATHERS.

To the evidence of the Apoftles may be added the authority of the Fathers, who fucceeded them. An appeal however to them, after fuch fuperiour evidence, may feem

unnecef-

unneceffary. But as it has been by fome
thought, that the writers in the firft æras
of Chriftianity have nothing to this purpofe,
I will proceed fomewhat farther, and fhew,
that they afford much intelligence upon
thefe articles, and of the greateft confequence. To this it has been urged, that, if
any doctrine is not to be found in the
apoftolick Writings, no authority of the
Fathers can give it a fanction. This is very
true. But if a perfon through frailty and
mifconception fhould imagine, that any
article was of doubtful purport, and attended
with obfcurity, then the evidence of thofe,
who had converfed with the Apoftles and
their immediate difciples, muft have weight.
And thofe of the fecond century, who came
later, are ftill fufficiently early to have their
opinion admitted: more efpecially, if they are
unanimous, and wrote before any different
notion had taken place. To this we fhould
add the fituation of thofe, who at that period wrote upon this fubject. For from this
circumftance an argument of confequence
may be deduced, of which I have elfewhere
availed

availed myfelf. They are found to have lived at fuch a diftance from each other, that, had any error fo early crept into the church in one region, it could not fo foon have reached to another, much lefs to all. The church of Alexandria had little communication with that of Carthage, and was ftill farther feparated from Lyons. And the profelytes at Lyons had as little correfpondence with thofe at Edeffa, Antioch, and Samaria. The unanimity therefore of writers, thus unconnected, fhews the truth of the doctrine: and if any further proof is wanting, they certainly afford it. The evidence of the Fathers will afcertain this truth: which evidence has been quoted more or lefs by various writers under different arrangements. I will however venture to introduce it again, and at large. I will alfo add, what feems to have been omitted; and place the whole in the moft true and proper light to the very beft of my power.

OF THE DOCTRINE OF THE HOLY TRINITY.

JUSTIN MARTYR.

He fays, that the Chriftians were reputed
Atheifts ; and confeffes, that they were really
fo in refpect to the gods of the Gentiles —
¹αλλ' υχι τυ αληθεςατυ, και Πατρος δικαιοσυνης
και σωφροσυνης και των αλλων αρετων, ανεπιμικτυ
τε κακιας, Θευ. Αλλ' εκεινον τε, και τον παρ'
αυτυ υιον ελθοντα και διδαξαντα ήμας ταυτα, και
τον των αλλων επομενων, και εξομοιυμενων, αγαθων
Αγγελων ςρατον. Πνευμα τε το προφητικον σεβο-
μεθα, και προσκυνυμεν, λογω και αληθεια τιμωντες,
και παντι βυλομενω μαθειν, ως εδιδαχθημεν, αφ-
θονως παραδιδοντες. *But we are not Atheifts in
refpect to the moft true God, the Father of all
righteoufnefs and wifdom, and of every other virtue,
without the leaft mixture of depravity. For we
reverence and worfhip both Him, and his Son,
who proceeded from Him; and who afforded us
this knowledge (of God and Chrift), and afforded
the fame to the whole hoft of his excellent mef-
fengers,*

---

¹ Apologia prima, p. 6.

fengers, the good angels, who miniſter to Him, and are made like Him. We likewiſe reverence and adore that Spirit, from which proceedeth all prophecy; affording towards it a true and rational worſhip. And we are ready to impart freely to all, who are willing to be inſtruɛted, the ſame information, that we have received.

I can give you (ſays Juſtin[1]) *another proof from the Scriptures* (concerning Chriſt), *that God in the beginning, before all the worlds, produced from himſelf a certain intelleɛtual power; which is by the Holy Spirit* (in the Scriptures) *mentioned, as the Son* (of God), *as Wiſdom, as an Angel, as God; and ſome-times as the Lord, and the Logos, or Word.* Μαρτυριον δε και αλλο ὑμιν απο των γραφων δωσω· ὁτι αρχην προ παντων των κτισματων ὁ Θεος γε-γεννηκε δυναμιν τινα εξ ἑαυτȣ λογικην, ἡτις και δοξα κυριȣ ὑπο τȣ πνευματος τȣ ἁγιȣ καλειται, ποτε δε Υἱος, ποτε δε Σοφια, ποτε δε Αγγελος, ποτε δε Θεος, ποτε δε Κυριος, και Λογος. Juſtin Martyr was born in the beginning of the ſecond century ſoon after the death of St. John.

---

[1] Dialog. cum Tryph. p. 159. E.

ΛΤΗF·

ATHENAGORAS.

Athenagoras complains of the fame unjuſt
accuſation: and he ſays — *How muſt any body
be aſtoniſhed, when he hears us accuſed of
Atheiſm, who acknowledge God the Father,
and God the Son, together with the Holy Spirit;
and maintain their power comprehended in
unity, and their difference in reſpect to perſon-
ality and order.* I give, what I think, is
the true purport, which ſometimes cannot be
expreſſed, but by a periphraſis. The original
is, as follows. [1] Τις ɤν ɤκ αν απορησαι, λε-
γοντας Θεον Πατερα, και υιον Θεον, και πνευμα
ἁγιον, δεικνυντας αυτων και την εν τη ἑνωσει δυναμιν,
και την εν τη ταξει διαιρεσιν, ακɤσας Αθɤɤς καλɤ-
μενɤς; He had before ſaid — εςιν ὁ υιος τɤ
Θεɤ Λογος τɤ Πατρος εν ιδεα και ενεργεια.
Προς αυτɤ γαρ και δι᾽ αυτɤ παντα εγενετο, ἑνος
οντος τɤ Πατρος και τɤ υιɤ.[2] *The Son of God
is*

is the *Word of the Father, the same in compre-*
hension, and operation. For through *Him, and*
by Him were all things created; the Son and
the Father being one. He then mentions, that
it is the duty of man to confider this myftery — Τις ἡ τȣ παιδος προς τον Πατερα ἑνοτης,
τις ἡ τȣ Πατρος προς τον υἱον κοινωνια, τι το
Πνευμα, τις ἡ των τοσȣτων ἑνωσις, και διαιρεσις
ἑνȣμενων, τȣ Πνευματος, τȣ Παιδος, τȣ Πατρος ——
What is that unity between the Son and the
Father; and what the communion of the Father
with the Son: Alfo to fearch — *What is the*
Spirit: and to confider — *The Union of thefe*
wonderful Beings, and their difference, when
united, the Holy Spirit, the Son, and the
Father.

E   THEOPHILUS.

THEOPHILUS OF ANTIOCH.

He mentions, that the Word proceeded from God before the worlds; and that all things were created by him. Τετον τον Λογον εσχεν ὑπεργον των ὑπ' αυτε γεγενημενων, και δι' αυτε τα παντα πεποιηκεν.[1] This learned Father was, like many others, too much tinctured with the Platonick philofophy, and alfo with a degree of myfticifm, which began very early to prevail in the church; yet he fpeaks to the purpofe. Και αἱ Τρεις ἡμεραι . . . . . τυποι εισιν της Τριαδος, τε Θεε, και τε Λογε αυτε, και της Σοφιας αυτε. Thefe three days (of the creation) are Types of the Trias, The Father, the Son, and his Spirit of Wifdom. Though he is in fome places much too fanciful in his illuftrations, yet he affords us the fenfe of the church in his time about this great article of religion: and he wrote about the middle of the fecond century.

[1] Ad Autolyc. L. ii. p. 355. B.

[2] Ibid. p. 360. E.

TATIANUS.

TATIANUS.

This learned Father was fomewhat antecedent to Athenagoras, and a difciple of
Juftin Martyr; in whofe time he became a
convert to Chriftianity. He fpeaks of the
Word, as — εργον πρωτοτοκον τȣ Πατρος — *the
firft inftance of the productive power of God.*
Γεγονε δε κατα μερισμον, ȣ κατ' αποκοπην. *This
was effected by a divifion, but without feparation.*[1] Τȣτον ισμεν τȣ Κȣσμȣ την αρχην. *We
know that he was the head and origin of all
things.* Ὁ μεν ȣν Λογος προ της των ανδρων
κατασκευης Αγγελων δημιȣργος γινεται. *The
Word before the formation of man created the
angels in heaven.* Ὁ Λογος, κατ' εικονα Θεȣ γε-
γονως— *the Word, which was the image of God.*[2]

[1] Orat. cont. Græcos, p. 247.

[2] Ibid. p 249.

IRENÆUS.

IRENÆUS.

IIe is faid to have been born in the reign of Trajan, towards the beginning of the fecond century. Some think, that he was not quite fo early. It is certain that he had been a difciple of Pothinus; and alfo of Polycarp, who had been a difciple of Saint John. The former he fucceeded as bifhop of Lyons, where he afterwards fuffered martyrdom. •

He mentions the unity of the Holy Spirit with Chrift, and at the fame time their unity with the Father — την προς αλληλυς άμα, και την προς τον Πατερα ένωσιν.[1] He fpeaks of Chrift as the Son of God — Solus vere Magifter Dominus nofter, et 'bonus vere Filius Dei . . . Verbum Dei Patris;[2] and fays, that he always was with the Father — Filius Patris . . . qui ab initio eft cum Patre.[3]

always

[1] Adver. Hæref. L. i. p. 39. l. 30.

—always one and the fame God — femper
eundum Deum [1] — Deus, et Dominus, et
Rex æternus, et unigenitus.[2] Very numerous are the proofs to this purpofe, which
may be obtained from this refpeĉtable writer.
I fhall only mention an obfervation, which
he very juftly made — that neither Chrift
himfelf, nor the Holy Spirit, nor the Apoftles, would have declared a perfon, who had
no title to divinity, determinately and abfo-
lutely God, were it not founded in truth.[3]
To thefe may be added his words in another
place. Vere igitur cum Pater fit Dominus,
et Filius vere fit Dominus, merito Spiritus
Sanĉtus Domini appellatione fignavit eos.
And he has fhewn, that the Spirit of wifdom, which gives this teftimony, was Lord
alfo. By their co-operation all things were
made. Unus igitur Deus, qui Verbo et
Sapientiâ fecit, et adaptavit, omnia.[4]

---

[1] Adv. Hæref. L. iv. p. 364.   [2] Ib. L. iii. p. 249.

[3] Ib. L. iii. p. 208.

[4] Ib. L. iv. p. 331. See alfo p. 380. l. 2.

CLEMENS

CLEMENS OF ROME, AND CLEMENS OF
ALEXANDRIA.

Clemens Romanus was of the firft century, and fo early in it, as to have converfed
with Saint Peter, and other of the firft Dif
ciples. He has tranfmitted a brief, but very
comprehenfive, account of his faith; the fame
undoubtedly, which he had from his great
Mafters. Ουχ᾽ ἑνα Θεον εχομεν, και ἑνα Χριςον,
και ἑν πνευμα ... το εκχυθεν εφ᾽ ἡμας; *Have we
not One God, One Chriſt, and one Spirit,
whoſe divine influence is poured upon us?*[1]

Clemens of Alexandria fucceeded in time
to thofe above, and preferved the fame doctrines : and he fpeaks of Chrift, as the Logos,
and fays — Ἡ μεν γαρ τε Θεε εικων ὁ Λογος
αυτε, και υἱος τε Νε γνησιος ὁ Θειος Λογος —*For
the Word of God is the image of God: and
that Holy Word is the genuine offspring of the
Divine*

---

[1] Epift. ad Corinth. 1. Sect. xlvi. p. 174.

Divine Intellect.[1] He in another place mentions the Τριας Ἁγια, the Sacred Trias, and ſpecifies the Father, Son, and Holy Spirit.[2]

TERTULLIAN:

AND THE OPINIONS OF THE ANCIENT PHILOSOPHERS.

Tertullian was later, than any of the writers already mentioned; and is ſuppoſed to have been converted to Chriſtianity about the year 196. He corroborates their teſtimony; and ſhews that the ſame doctrine, which prevailed in the eaſt and weſt, and at Rome, was maintained at Carthage, where he was born. This is ſhewn in the account, which he gives of this myſtery. Quod de Deo profectum eſt, Deus eſt, et Dei Filius, et Unus ambo: ita et de Spiritu Spiritus, et de Deo Deus.[3]

— Hic

---

[1] Cohort. V. i. p. 78. [2] Strom. L. v. V. ii. p. 710,

[3] Apologet. p. 20.

— Hic (Chriftus) acceptum a Patre munus effudit Spiritum Sanctum, tertium nomen Divinitatis, et tertium gradum Majeftatis ... et deductorem omnis veritatis, quæ eft in Patre, et Filio, et Spiritu Sancto fecundum Chriftianum facramentum.[1]

These truths, he fays, were in fome degree known to the Grecian philofophers. Apud veftros quoque Sapientes, Λογον, id eft, Sermonem, atque Rationem, conflat artificem videri univerfitatis.[2] They certainly were not totally ignorant of this truth. But they refined upon it, and introduced *Matter*, as part of the Trias, and as eternal. From the account given by Diogenes Laertius of Plato, one would imagine, that he allowed only two firft principles. [3] Δυο δε των παντων απεφηνεν αρχας, Θεον και 'Υλην, ον και Νεν προσαγορευει, και Αιτιον. *Plato declared, that the two principles of all things were God and Matter, which he ftyles the Mind, and the efficient Caufe.* But others give a better account

of

---

[1] Adver. Prax. p. 518.   [2] Apologet. p. 19.

of Plato's opinion. [1] Ταυτα οἱ τον Πλατωνα διασαφειν πειρωμενοι, επι τον πρωτον Θεον ανα-γεσιν, επι τε τον δευτρον Αιτιον, και τριτον την τε Κοσμε Ψυχην. The fame was expreffed under different names, of which Plutarch affords an example. [2] Σωκρατης Σωφρονισκε Αθηναιος, και Πλατων Αριςωνος Αθηναιος . . . . τρεις αρχας, τον Θεον, την Ὑλην, την Ιδεαν. *We find that Socrates, as well as Plato, held three Principles; which are ftyled, God, Matter, and Idea.* This laft is explained by Plato fomewhat differently. [3] Ἡ δε Ιδεα, εννοημα τε Θεε, ὁπερ ὁι Βαρβαροι Λογον ειρηκασι τε Θεε. *The Idea is the Intellect, or Wifdom of the Deity, which foreigners call the Logos, or Word of God.*

Juftin

---

[1] Eufeb. Præp. Evang. L xi. C. xx. p. 541.

Πορφυριος γαρ φησι, Πλατωνος εκτιθεμειος δοξαι, αχρι τριων ὑπογασιων την τε Θειε προελθειν εσιαι, ειναι δε τον μεν ανωτατω Θεον ταγαθον· μετ' αυτου δε και δευτερον τον δημιεργον· τριτον δε και την τε Κοσμε ψυχην. Cyril. Alex. cont. Jul. L. i. V. vi. p. 34.

[2] De Placitis Philof. L. i. p. 878.

[3] Clem. Alex. Strom. L. v. V. ii, p. 654.

Juftin Martyr makes the Trias of this philofopher to contain —[1] Θεον, και Ὑλην, και Ειδος—*God, Matter, and Image or Refemblance,* the fame as Idea. In moft of which examples, as I faid before, *Matter* is introduced as a firft principle, and eternal.

The doctrines, which we have been confidering, were not the difcoveries of Plato, but ORIGINAL TRUTHS,[2] differently modified and mifapplied by him in his writings. He intimates himfelf indeed, that they were not his own — ὁι βαρβαροι ειρηκασι. Let us then inquire, from what fource he derived them. Now, there was no nation, to which he had accefs, and from which alfo he could have obtained them, excepting the Jews. It is true,

---

[1] Ὁ γαρ Πλατων ποτε μεν τρεις αρχας τα παντος ειναι λεγει, Θεον, και Ὑλην, και Ειδος. Cohort. p. 12.

[2] Πλατων δι ὁ φιλοσοφος εκ των Μωσεως — ωφεληθεις. Clem. Alex. Strom. L. i. V. i. p. 419. See alfo p. 60, 176, 355. Αρα σοι δοκει ταυτα λεγων ὁ Πλατων τοις Ἑβραιων επηκολυθηκεναι δογμασι, Eufeb. Præp. Evang. L. xi. p. 534, and 51c.

true, that even this people had no perfect
and precife knowledge of thefe articles; yet
they had fufficient to improve heathenifm,
and to inftruct the divine Plato. And
whereas he fays, that, what he expreffed
Εννοημα, or *Intellect*, foreigners (οι Βαρβαροι)
ftyled Λογος, or the Word, or Reafon, none
but the Helleniftick Jews could have given
it this appellation. For I imagine the meaning of Plato to be, when he mentions — οπερ
οι Βαρβαροι Λογον ειρηκασι — that the people, to
whom he alludes, expreffed it literally by this
name. No people, but the Jews, had any
knowledge of a fecond Divine Being of fo
high an order and character: and none but
the Jews in Egypt could have rendered in
this manner Λογος. That they rendered it
in this manner may be feen by the Greek
verfion of the Bible. For though this verfion
was not made till after the time of Plato,
yet we may reafonably infer, that the term
Word, as a Perfon in Scripture, was antecedently thus expreffed by the Helleniftick
Jews in thofe parts.

THEIR EVIDENCE, OF GREAT CONSEQUENCE.

The Platonifts, and other Philofophers, who admitted thefe truths, were not uniform in their defcription, nor confiftent in their explanation. However, when they fpeak of a Trias, which confifted of Three αρχαι, or original ruling principles; and when they defcribe the Firft, as Θεος, God, the Second as Νες, Reafon, the fame as the Λογος, or divine *Word*; (which they fometimes do) and when they add a Third co-exifting Being, which they ftyle Σοφια, ψυχη τε Κοσμε, *Divine Wifdom, the Soul of the world*, they adopt articles of great confequence. We know too well, how fuch a belief in thefe times is oppofed, and denyed, as impious, and idolatrous, and contrary to religion, and reafon. Yet the perfons, of whom I have been fpeaking, embraced them, as foon as they had any knowledge of them, and faw their propriety and truth. And who were they, who gave this fanction to the .

doctrines above? Some of the wifeſt men,
that the world ever beheld; who laboured
moſt after true ſcience; and made the greateſt
advances towards virtue, and the knowledge
of God. We have no inſtances of the
powers of man, unaſſiſted from above,
proceeding ſo far. They ſaw a fitneſs and
propriety, where it is now denyed. Of this
illuſtrious band I ſhall mention only four;
Socrates, Plato, Ariſtotle, and Zeno. If
Philo Judeus went beyond them, it was,
becauſe he applied to a more ample ſource
of divine knowledge, afforded by a later
revelation.

We have ſeen, that, from the time that
this revelation took place, that is, from the
time of the Apoſtles, to the end of the ſecond century, in whatever region a Chriſtian
church was eſtabliſhed, a Sacred Trias was
univerſally admitted. Hence I make this
inference, that, if an error of this ſort had
ariſen ſo early, yet it could not equally have
prevailed in ſo many remote parts of the
world. And I proceed further, and am perſuaded,

fuaded, that this doctrine is fo little obvious
to the notions of mankind, that it could
fcarcely have been devifed by the fancy of man;
and if devifed, ftill, as I have before faid, it
could not have been fo univerfally propa-
gated. It has now prevailed for ages: and
we receive and maintain it, not in confequence
of any private and partial opinion; but
becaufe it is accompanied with, and enforced
by, a divine fanction; and has the uniform
fuffrage of the wifeft of men, who have alfo
tranfmitted it to us. We may be certain,
that there is in it nothing contrary to reafon,
by thofe great mafters of reafoning among
the Grecians fo readily adopting it. Philo
went far beyond them, as he had better
opportunities of information. Though no
friend to Chriftianity, he has admitted moft
of the principal doctrines, which relate to
the two characters of our Saviour. And
though he in fome refpects mifapplies them;
yet he plainly admits, and maintains
them. He was followed by thofe, who
fucceffively belonged to the fchool of
Alexandria: fuch as Plotinus, Porphyry,
and

and Proclus. They were men of great learning, and bitter enemies to Chriftianity; yet maintained the doctrines above. Thefe they borrowed, not from Plato, nor Pythagoras; whofe knowledge of them was limited, imperfect, and diffimilar; but from the Gofpel itfelf, where only they were fo amply to be found. Thefe, though beyond human apprehenfion, they admitted, becaufe they thought them divine truths, and confiftent with reafon.

They have been likewife maintained by fome of the moft learned among the Jews; however implacable enemies they might be to Chriftianity. The doctrine of the Meffias they admitted; and mentioned him, as the Word of God, and as God, antecedent to angels, and before creation. This appears from their Targums, and other Rabbinical writings: of which [1] P. Galatini gives a large account.

---

[1] P. Galatini de Arcanis Catholicæ Veritatis, L. i. C. iii. p. 8. L. ii. C. i. p. 41. E. L. iii. C. v. p. 118. L. iii. p. 136. E. L. ii. p. 47. B. 49. F. For a fight

account. Hence we learn, that thofe myfterious truths concerning the fecond Perfon,
which in thefe times are rejected by many
Chriftians, as impious, and idolatrous, were
allowed by the very people, who were the
greateft enemies to idolatry, and who always
fhewed themfelves the moft hoftile to Chriftianity and the Gofpel. They maintained
them, as being, when made known, confonant to reafon, and as having the fanction
of the Scriptures.

of this Treatife, from whence I have made thefe inferences, I am indebted to my moft learned and excellent
Friend, the Lord Bifhop of Salifbury.

PART II.

PARTICULAR DOCTRINES MAINTAINED BY PHILO.

FROM HIS OWN WORDS.

OF THE IMPURITY OF OUR NATURE.

ΤΗΣ γαρ ακαθαρσιας ἡμων εν μεσω φησι την σκηνην ἱδρυσασθαι το Λογιον, ἱνα εχωμεν ᾡ καθαρθησομεθα, εκνιψαμενοι και απολυσαμενοι τα καταῤῥυπαινοντα ἡμων τον αθλιον, και δυσκλειας γεμοντα, βιον.[1]

For

[1] Quis Rer. Div. Hæres. Vol. 1. p. 488. l. 44.

For the Scripture informs us, that it pleafed God to fix the tabernacle of his oracle in the midft of our impurities; that we might have an opportunity of being cleanfed, by wafhing away all thofe fordes, with which the wretched and bafe conftitution of man abounds.

He feems here to allude to a paffage of Saint Paul, who mentions the High Prieft, that is *fet on the right hand of the throne of the Majefty in the Heavens —A Minifter of the fanctuary, and of the true tabernacle, which the Lord pitched, and not man.*[1] *. . . Which ftood only in meats, and drinks, and divers wafhings, and carnal ordinances;*[2] and which in the Book of Wifdom is ftyled — *a refemblance of the Holy Tabernacle, which thou haft prepared from the beginning.*[3]

[1] Heb. viii. 1, 2.   [2] Heb. ix. 10.

[3] Wifdom ix. 8.

OF THE INSUFFICIENCY OF MAN WITHOUT DIVINE ASSISTANCE.

He had been fpeaking of την καθαρσιν της ψυχης, *the purification of the foul*, and then adds — παραχωρυντας τω θεω το φαιδρυνειν, και μηδεποτε νομισαντας ικανυς ειναι εαυτυς ανευ θειας επιφροσυνης των κηλιδων αναμεσον εκνιψαι και απολυσαι βιον[1] — *Which foul we muft leave to God to brighten; and by no means think, that we of ourfelves are able without the grace of God to wafh and cleanfe our mortal frame from the fpots and ftains, with which it abounds.*

He enumerates in another place fome of the moft crying fins — μοιχειας, ανδροφονιας, κλοπης, ψευδομαρτυριας, επιθυμιας — αμαρτηματα[2] — *The crimes of adultery, murder, theft, bearing falfe witnefs, evil concupifcenfe — offences in general.*

[1] De Somniis. V. i. p. 662. l. 37.

[2] Quis Rer. Divin. Hæres. V. i. p. 497. l. 22.

OF PROPITIATION.

He fpeaks of propitiation, which he ftyles, like [1] St. John, ιλασμος; and feems to have fome faint allufions, not only to original fin, but alfo to our renovation through the Word of God. Τετ' εςιν αφεσις, τετ' ελευθερια παντελης ψυχης, ὁν επλανηθη τε πλανον αποσειομενης, και προς την απλανη φυσιν μεθορμιζομενης, και επι τας κληρας επανιτσης, ἑς ελαχεν, ἡνικα λαμπρον επνει, και τοις περι των καλων πονοις ηνθει. Τοτε γαρ αυτην των αθλων αγαμενος ὁ Ἱερος Λογος ετιμησε, γερας εξαιρετον δες, κληρον αθανατον, την εν αφθαρτω γενει ταξιν.[2] *This is remiffion* (of fins), *this the compleat freedom of the foul: when it gets free from that error, in which it was bewildered, and labours after that blamelefs nature, and that happy lot,*
                                                                    which

---

[1] Και αιτος (Χριτος) ιλασμος ιςι περι των αμαρτιων ἡμων. 1 John ii. 2. By Saint Paul it is called ιλαςηριον.—Ὁν προιθετο ὁ Θεος ιλαςηριον δια της πιςεως εν τω αυτε αιματι ... δια την παρεσιν των προγιγονοταν αμαρτηματων. Rom. iii. 25.

[2] De Congreffu. V. i. p. 534, 535.

which it once had, when it breathed virtue,
and flourished in good works. Then the Holy
Word of God, being highly pleased with it's
noble endeavours, honours these efforts, and in
consequence of them affords it a most excellent
reward, a title to immortality, and a portion
among those beings, which are no longer cor-
ruptible. This in the language of Scripture
is —Among *the souls of just men made perfect.*
Such perfons are in another place defcribed
by Philo, as — των ασωματων και θειων πραγματων κληρονομοι [1]—*Heirs of spiritual and di-*
vine advantages.

OF A MEDIATOR, AND OF FAITH.

An account is given in Numbers xvi. 46.
of a fearful plague, which enfued upon the
rebellion of Korah; when fourteen thoufand
and feven hundred of the people were con-
fumed; and more were in danger. But
Mofes

---

[1] Philo. Vol. i. p. 482. l. 3. Alfo p. 473.

Mofes faid unto Aaron, Take a cenfer, and put fire therein from off the altar, and put on incenfe, and go quickly unto the congregation, and make an atonement for them. And he (Aaron, the High Prieft) *flood between the dead and the living, and the plague was flayed.* Philo faw clearly, that this interceffion of Aaron was a type of the mediation of the Great High Prieft, whom he acknowledges to be the Logos, or Word of God.[1] He accordingly in another place gives a very particular character of the Divine Word, and his mediatorial power, which he deduces from the hiftory above. Τω δε Αρχαγγελω και πρεσβυτατω Λογω δωρεαν εξαιρετον εδωκεν ο τα ολα γεννησας πατηρ, ινα μεθοριος ςας το γενομενον διακρινη τε πεποιηκοτος. Ὁ δ' αυτος ικετης μεν εςι τε θνητε κηραινοντος αει προς το φθαρτον, πρεσβευτης δε τε Ἡγεμονος προς το υπηκοον. Αγαλλεται δε επι τη δωρεα, και σεμνυνομενος αυτην εκδιηγειται φασκων — Καγω ειςηκειν ανα μεσον Κυριε και υμων' ετε αγεννητος ως ο Θεος ων, ετε γεννητος ως υμεις, αλλα μεσος των ακρων, αμφο-

τεροις

τεροις ὁμηρευων. παρα μεν τῳ φυτευσαντι, προς
πιςιν τε μη συμπαν αφανισαι ποτε και αποςηναι
το γενος, ακοσμιαν αντι κοσμε ἑλομενον· παρα δε
τῳ φυντι, προς ευελπιςιαν τε μηποτε τον ἱλεων
Θεον περιϊδειν το ιδιον εργον. Εγω γαρ επικηρυ-
κευσομαι τα ειρηναια γενεσει παρα τε καθαιρειν
πολεμες εγνωκοτος, ειρηνοφυλακος αει Θεε.[1] *The
Great Father of all gave this extraordinary
gift to that most ancient, and Principal, of all
Angels, his Holy Word, that he should stand
mid-way, and separate the creature from the
Creator. This Word* (the Logos) *is accordingly the Intercessor for mortal man, who is
always tending to corruption: and he is appointed a Messenger and Legate from the
Supreme Lord to his subjects. This office is
highly acceptable to him; and he shews the
dignity of it, when he is introduced, saying,* (at
the rebellion of Korah) " *It was I, who stood*
(a Mediator) *between you, and the Lord.*" *For
he is not unbegotten like God; nor created like
man; but a medium between the extremes,*
bordering

[1] Quis Rer. Divin. Hæres. V. i. p. 501, 502,
See also V, i. p. 689, 690.

F 4.

bordering upon each. So that, in respect to the Creator, he is able to obtain assurance, that he will never ruin, nor reject, the race of man; nor, instead of order, suffer the world to lapse into anarchy: and in respect to the creature, that he may by faith be certified of this truth, that the God of all mercies will never neglect the work of his hands. I therefore, (says the Word of God) *proclaim peace to all the world from that Power, who maketh wars to cease; from God, who is the guardian of peace.* In which passage mention is made, not only of a Mediator between God and man, but also of a good hope, or confidence in God — προς ευελπιϛιαν, κ.τ.λ. — of an assurance, of a FAITH, or trust in the Creator — προς ϖιϛιν, κ.τ.λ. — grounded on the Mediator's intercession.

OF REPENTANCE, AND NEWNESS OF LIFE.

These, says Philo, are consequent upon Faith and Hope. Δευτεραν δ'εχει ταξιν, μετα την ελπιδα, ἡ επι τοις αμαρτανομενοις

6

ϖξχνοια

μετανοια και βελτιωσις[1]—*In the next place,
after hope, comes repentance of all our sins,
and newness of life.* The like occurs in
another place. Μετα δε την ελπιδος νικην, αγων
δευτερος εςιν, εν ω μετανοια αγωνιζεται[2]—*After
the victory gained by hope, another conflict
comes on, in which repentance is engaged.*
And he afterwards alludes to the severity of
these conflicts — μετα δε τες της μετανοιας
αγωνας[3]— *these struggles of a penitent heart.*

In the Treatise de Execrationibus, he
mentions the curses denounced upon the
wicked. But if there be such, who repent,
and will confess their sins — ὁμολογησαντες ὁσα
ἡμαρτον — and will endeavour after a better
way of life — ευμενειας τευξονται της εκ τε
Σωτηρος και ἱλεω Θεε[4]— *they will obtain favour
from the Saviour, and God of all mercy.* We
are

---

[1] De Abrahamo. V. ii. p. 3. l. 46.

[2] De Præmiis et Pœnis. V. ii. p. 410. l. 36.

[3] Ibid. p. 411. l. 36.

[4] Ibid. V. ii. p. 435. l. 35.

are then entitled to be the children of the
moſt High; and our ſins are forgiven
through him — τον Αγγελον, ὁς εςι Λογος,
ὡσπερ Ιατρον κακων [1]—*that Angel, the Word of
God, who is the phyſician and healer of all our
evils.* For we cannot pleaſe God of ourſelves: even our beſt actions are not truly
acceptable — μηδε την αρετην, ανευ θειας επιφροσυνης, ἱκανην εξ ἑαυτης ωφελειν ειναι [2] — *Even
virtue itſelf without the divine ſanction can
have no merit, nor advantage.* All theſe good
things are accompliſhed by the Word, ſtyled
the great High Prieſt, the Son of God, τον
Λογον Θειον. Ὁ δε αυτος ἱκετης τε θνητε. *And
he is the Interceſſor for mortal man.* Hence
he is mentioned as Μεσος, and Μεθοριος, *the
Mediator,* and as *bordering upon both*; by
whom we are made υἱοι Θεε ανθρωποι — *ſons
of God;* και θειων πραγματων κληρονομοι — *and
heirs of heavenly advantages.*

---

[1] De Leg. Alleg. V. i. p. 122. l. 17.

[2] Ibid. p. 203. l. 18.

OF FREEDOM BY THE DEATH OF THE HIGH PRIEST.

I have mentioned, that Philo was very much embarrassed about that part of the Law, wherein it was said, that the man of guilt should fly to an appointed city of refuge; and not be acquitted till the death of the High Priest. Τεταρτον και λοιπον ην των προταθεντων, ἡ προθεσμια της των πεφευγοτων καθοδȣ, τȣ Αρχιερεως ὁ Θανατος, πολλην εν τω ῥητω μοι παρεχȣσα δυσκολιαν. Ανισος γαρ ἡ τιμωρια κατα των τα αυτα δρασαντων νομοθετειται, ειγε ὁι μεν πλειω χρονον αποδρασονται, ὁι δε ελαττω. Μακροβιωτατοι γαρ, ὁι δε ολιγοχρονιωτατοι των Αρχιερεων εισι. Και ὁι μεν νεοι, ὁι δε πρεσβυται καθιϛανται. Και των εαλωκοτων επ᾽ ακȣσιω φονω, ὁι μεν εν αρχη της ἱερωσυνης εφυγαδευθησαν, ὁι δ᾽ ηδη μελλοντος τελευταν τȣ ἱερωμενȣ[1]—*The fourth remaining article of these propositions, is the ordinance concerning the return of those, who had fled for refuge, which*

was

---

[1] De Profugis. V. i. p. 561, 562.

*was to be at the death of the High Prieſt.
The conſideration of this has given me a good
deal of trouble from the purport. For the pu-
niſhment appointed is not equally diſtributed;
as ſome muſt have been confined for a longer,
and ſome for a ſhorter, ſeaſon; and as ſome of
the High Prieſts were of a longer, others of a
ſhorter, date; and ſome arrive at the dignity
when young, others when old. And thoſe, who
were accidentally guilty of bloodſhed muſt have
ſought this ſhelter, ſome at the beginning of the
prieſthood, and others when the High Prieſt
was near his death.* Theſe were the difficulties, which gave Philo ſo much uneaſi-
neſs, and which for a time he could not
ſolve. But he ſays, that at laſt he perceived
it to be typical, and a myſtery. Λεγομεν
γαρ, τον Αρχιερεα εκ ανθρωπον, αλλα Λογον Θειον
ειναι, παντων εχ εκεσιων μονον, αλλα και ακεσιων
αδικηματων αμετοχον ... διοτι, οιμαι, γονεων αφθαρ-
των και καθαρωτατων ελαχεν, Πατρος μεν Θεε, ὁς
και των συμπαντων εςι πατηρ· Μητρος δε Σοφιας,
δι᾽ ἡς τα ὁλα ηλθεν εις γενεσιν.' *I maintain then,
that*

De P... V ... . 13.

*that the High Priest, alluded to, is not a man,
but the Sacred Logos, the Word of God: who
is incapable of either voluntary or involuntary
fin. I therefore conclude, that he was born of
Parents the moft pure and incorruptible; having
for his Father, God, who is the Author of all
things; and Divine Wifdom for his Mother,
by whom all things came into being.* Και διοτι
την κεφαλην κεχρισαι ελαιω[1]— *and upon this account he is faid to have his head anointed with
oil.* Who would think, that, when he faw
fo much, he would not have feen more?
that he fhould not have perceived the Meffiah
Chrift, the anointed of God, fo often mentioned in the Prophets, here clearly pointed
out? He concludes — Ταυτα δ' εκ απο σκοπε
μοι λελεκται, αλλ' υπερ τε διδαξαι, οτι φυσικω-
τατη προθεσμια καθοδε φυγαδων, ο τε Αρχιερεως
εςι θανατος[2]—*Thefe things I have not mentioned
without good reafon: but to fhew, that the
natural and appointed return of the fugitives*

was

---

[1] De Profugis. V. i. p. 562. l. 22.

[2] Ibid. p. 563. l. 24.

was the death of the High Priest: whom he
ftyles ἱερωτατος Λογος — *the moſt Holy Word of
God.* But this death he allegorizes, and by
refinement ruins the whole.

THE SOURCE, FROM WHENCE HE
BORROWED HIS OPINIONS.

Such were the opinions of Philo Judeus
upon thefe very interefting fubjects: and we
have feen the reafons given by him, which
are very numerous, and at the fame time
equally fignificant. The only queftion is,
from whence he could obtain them. From
Plato and his difciples little to this purpofe
could have been derived: and many of thefe
truths could not have been obtained by him,
even from his brethren the Jews, and their
facred writings, excepting fome few intimations. Thefe have fince been made obvious and clear by a later revelation. There
was therefore no fource, to which he could
poffibly have applied, but to the Apoftles,
and Evangelifts, and other difciples of Chrift.

It

It has been afferted, that he was born much too early to be inftructed by them. But this is fpoken without fufficient grounds. In the firft place, we know nothing precifely concerning his birth. And fecondly, we are certified by his own evidence of this, that he went ambaffadour from Alexandria to Rome in the fourth year of Caligula, which was in the year of the Chriftian Æra 42. And if he were of this age at the time of his embaffy, he muft have been coæval with our Saviour[1]: and as he lived to the reign of Nero, we may be affured, that he furvived Chrift many years. At all rates he muft have been in a ftate of manhood during the miniftry of Chrift; and confequently faw numbers of his followers for many years afterwards; and, if we may judge by his doctrines, was acquainted with the Gofpels, and with the Epiftles of Saint Paul.

---

[1] If he were born fome years before the birth of Chrift, as fome have infifted, ftill he muft have been contemporary with Chrift during his whole refidence on earth: for he certainly furvived him many years.

Paul. Saint Mark, the firſt biſhop of
Alexandria, could not have been unknown
to him. Theſe things, I think, are in a
great degree evident from the internal evidence of the doɛtrines, which he has tranſmitted. For there is only this alternative.
He muſt either have borrowed theſe truths
from the ſource mentioned; or he muſt
have had them by inſpiration. But to ſo
great an indulgence he ſeems to have had
no pretence: he conſequently received them
from the Apoſtles, and the firſt proſelytes
to the Goſpel. The very words, in which
thoſe doɛtrines are delivered, ſhew it.

INFERENCES.

Nor was it Philo only, who took theſe
advantages. He ſet an early example. And
the Pagan world at large was ſoon improved
by the doɛtrines of Chriſtianity. The wiſeſt
of the Philoſophers ſaw it's ſuperiority. And
though they held the people in contempt,
from

from among whom it proceeded, and could
not be reconciled to it's great Author; yet
they borrowed their ethics from him, and
enriched their philofophy with truths unknown before. Many of them admitted the
very myfteries: and though they tried to
explain them each according to his particular
fancy; yet, I fay, they were admitted; and
not thought reprehenfible, nor contrary to
reafon. Theodoret takes notice, (Θεραπευτ. ϛ.)
that Plutarch, Numenius, and Plotinus,
borrowed from the facred writings. To
thefe might be added, Epictetus, Antoninus,
Porphyrius, Maximus Tyrius, Hierocles,
Proclus, with many more. The emperour
Julian, that bitter enemy, copied largely
from the fyftem, which he tried to ruin.
The lump of leaven, mentioned by our
Saviour, began very foon to operate upon
the mafs, in which it was inclofed; and proceeds at this day in it's operation. The good
effects of Chriftianity are felt far beyond it's
limits; and will in time be univerfal. That
they are fo extenfive at prefent, is owing in
no fmall degree to the writings of Philo.

G

FARTHER INFERENCES.

If thefe arguments, which I have deduced
from Philo, be true, as I truft they are, we
have in confequence of it the moft early
and decifive evidence in favour of the doctrine, with which we are engaged. And
we may be certified, if any proof be wanting, concerning the opinion of the firft
Chriftians and Apoftles, in refpect to this
myftery. The atteftation of the Fathers is
attended with great validity, and cannot be
fet afide. But this from Philo is ftill more
forcible and convincing, as it is more early.
And though it may not proceed from an
enemy, yet it certainly comes not from a
friend: fo that there could have been no
prejudice nor partiality in favour of the
articles mentioned. It is certain, that the
words of the Apoftles, and more efpecially
thofe of our Saviour, ftand in no need of
any foreign evidence to be authenticated.
But when in thefe times the purport of
thofe words is difputed, and the very doc-

z   trines

trines denied; and when the opinions of
the Fathers are efteemed either too late or
too indeterminate; then this prior evidence
of an Alien muft have weight. For the
truths, which he has advanced, he could
not unaffifted have obtained. The wifdom
of man could not have arrived at fuch
knowledge. He was therefore beholden to
others for this intelligence: and I have
fhewn, to whom he was indebted : or rather
he has given a plain proof of it himfelf.
He drew from a noble fource: and the
famples, which he has produced, fhew, that
they are from the *well of wifdom*, from the
fpring *of living waters*, the *fountain of life*.
He drew indeed but partially; yet, what he
has afforded, is attended with great advantage.

THE

THE MISAPPLICATION OF THESE GREAT
TRUTHS BY PHILO.

I have obferved, that Philo fpeaks only of
the divinity of the Logos, or Word of
God; and induftrioufly avoids taking notice of the Meffiah, the Anointed of God;
by the Apoftles and Evangelifts called Chrift.
But though he tacitly denies the humanity
of our Saviour; yet he has taken almoft
every attribute, which belongs to Chrift,
the Son of man, and refers them to him in
his prior, and heavenly, ftate. But with
this part of his character they are not confiftent. He therefore unduly adjudges to
the Logos, as reprefented in his Writings,
the feveral offices [1] of High Prieft, to make
an atonement; [2] of Meffenger from the
Deity, to declare his will to mankind;
                                        of

[1] Philo. V. i. p. 653. ὡς ὁ κοσμος, εν ﹐ και αρχιερευς, ὁ
σρωτογονος αυτη θειος Λογι,.

[2] Id. V. i. p. 501. Πρεσβευτης τυ ἡγεμονο; προς το ὑπηκοον.

[1] of Mediator between God and man, to supplicate in behalf of offenders and propitiate an offended Sovereign; [2] of Surety to each party; and [3] of Shepherd, delegated by the Moſt High to take care of his ſacred Flock. Reſtore theſe articles to the Meſſiah, to whom they particularly belong; and the opinions of Philo will be found in moſt inſtances very ſimilar to thoſe of the Apoſtles; and oftentimes the very ſame.

---

[1] Philo. V. i. p. 501, 502. Ἱκετης . . . τε διητε . . . προς το αφθαρτον.

[2] Ibid. αμφοτεροις ὁμηρευων.

[3] Id. V. i. p. 308. Ποιμην . . . ὁς την επιμελειαι της ἱερας ταυτης αγελης, οια τις μεγαλε βασιλεως ὑπαρχος, διαδεξεται.

UPON

UPON THE PASSAGE IN PHILO DE CONFU-
SIONE LING. V. I. P. 427. L. 3.

I have mentioned, that Philo fpeaks of
the Logos, or *Word of God*, as fometimes
bearing the likenefs of man — ὁ κατ᾽ εικονα
ανθρωπος.[1] The learned Editor thinks, that
this is not the right reading; for which he
fubftitutes — ὃ κατ᾽ εικονα ανθρωπος — *whofe
image man is*. For he imagines, that Philo
never could have allowed, that any fuch
fimilitude fubfifted. But in this, I think,
he is miftaken. In the firft place, we have
the authority of Eufebius for this reading,
who quotes the whole paffage; a part of
which is ὁ κατ᾽ εικονα ανθρωπος.[2] In the next
place, it is warranted by the context: which
would be injured by the alteration. Philo
is mentioning feveral characters and titles of
the — πρωτογονος υιος — *The firft begotten Son
of*

---

[1] De Confuf. Ling. V. i. p. 427. l. 6.

[2] Præp. Evangel. L. xi. c. 15. p. 533.

of God: as the — [1] Αρχαγγελος πολυωνυμος — *The Great Archangel under different appellations :* — αρχη, και ονομα Θεȣ, και Λογος, και ὁ κατ' εικονα ανθρωπος, και [2] ὁρων Ισραηλ — *The beginning or Creator of all things, the name of God* (Jehovah), *the Word of God, the likeneſs of man, and the Guardian of Iſrael.* If we tranſpoſe this, as our Editor adviſes, there is an article introduced in the moſt improper place, and in the moſt unneceſſary manner. The hiſtory relates to the different names and attributes of God's Firſt-born; and the likeneſs of man to Chriſt has here no place, nor connexion. The words are to be conſidered, as relating to one of the titles and attributes of the Son of God. The Logos in the Scriptures is deſcribed as appearing to Abraham, and to other Patriarchs, in a human form: and to this, I imagine, Philo alludes, when he ſays, ὁ κατ' εικονα ανθρωπος. This reading has the

---

[1] De Confuſ. Ling. V. i. p. 427. l. 4—7.

[2] He makes uſe of the word ὁρων in this ſenſe immediately afterwards — τȣ ὁρωντος ὁι ακȣοντες — *who obey their overſeer.* Ibid. l. 14.

G 4

the fanction of [1] Origen, who tells us, that Philo wrote, περι τε μη ως ανθρωπον λεγεσθαι ειναι τον Θεον. Philo in the page above-mentioned (V. i. p. 427) fays, that *man was born after the image of the Word*. There muft therefore have been, however partial, yet a reciprocal likenefs. [2]

[1] Origen in Matt. p. 477.

[2] Philo fays, there are two portions of the Scripture, which mention — ἐν μεν, ὁτι ἐκ ὡς ανθρωπος ὁ Θεος, ἑτερον δι, ὁτι ὡς ανθρωπος. Quod Deus fit Immut. V. i. p. 282, 283. And Quod a Deo, &c. p. 656.

A

A

RECAPITULATION

OF THE

CHARACTER AND ATTRIBUTES

OF THE

LOGOS,

WITH

THE COLLATERAL EVIDENCE FROM

SCRIPTURE.

ALSO

SOME FARTHER PARTICULAR DOCTRINES

BORROWED BY PHILO

FROM THE APOSTOLIC WRITINGS,

BUT MISAPPLIED.

RECAPITULATION.

I.

THE LOGOS IS

THE Son of God — Τον ορθον Λογον Θεε Ύιον —of a divine nature.[1] Πατρος (Θεε) Ύιος.[2] *The Son of God the Father.*

Mark i. 1.   Αρχη τε Ευαγγελιε Ιησε Χριςε, υιε τε Θεε.

The beginning of the Gospel of Jesus Chriſt the Son of God.

Luke iv. 41.   Συ ει ὁ Χριςος, ὁ υιος τε Θεε.
Thou art Chriſt, the Son of God.

Acts viii. 37.   Πιςευω τον υιον τε Θεε ειναι τον Ιησεν Χριςον.

I believe, that Jeſus Chriſt is the Son of God.

John i. 34.   Ὁυτος εςιν ὁ υιος τε Θεε.
This is the Son of God.

II. The

[1] De Agric. V. i. p. 308. l. 27.
[2] De Profugis, V. i. p. 562. l. 20. p. 414. 427. 437.

II.

The Second Divinity. Δευ]ερος Θεος ὁ Λογος.[1]
He may be esteemed the God of us
imperfect beings—ʽOυτος γαρ ἡμων των ατελων
αν ειη Θεος.[2]

John i. 1.   Και Θεος ην ὁ Λογος.
              And the Word (the Logos) *was
              God.*

1 Cor. i. 24. Χριςον, Θε8 δυναμιν, και Θε8 σοφιαν.
              *Christ the power of God, and the
              wisdom of God.*

III.

The first-begotten of God. Πρωτογονος
Θειος Λογος.[3] And the most ancient of all
beings— ὑιος πρεσβυτατος.[4]

Heb.

---

[1] Fragm. Vol. ii. p. 625.

[2] De Leg. Alleg. V. i. p. 128. l. 43.

[3] De Somniis, V. i. p. 653. l. 24.

[4] De Conf. Ling. V. i. p. 414. l. 20.

Heb. i. 6.   Ὁταν δε παλιν εισαγαγη τον Πρωτοτοκον εις την οικεμενην.

*And when he again bringeth his
Firſt-born into the world.*

Coloſ. i. 15.   Ὁς εςι . . . . . πρωτοτοκος πασης
κτισεως.

*The Logos — who is the firſt-
born of every creature.*

IV.

The Image and Likeneſs of God.   Εικων
τε Θεε.[1]   Λογος δε εςιν εικων Θεε.[2]

———————

Coloſſ. i. 15.   Εικων τε Θεε αορατε.

*Chriſt, the Image of the inviſible
God.*

Heb.

———

[1] De Mundi Opif. V. i. p. 6. l. 42. p. 414 419. 656.

[2] De Monarch. V. ii, p. 225. l. 26.

Heb. i. 3.   Απαυγασμα της δοξης, και χα-
ρακτηρ της ὑποςασεως αυτε (τε
Θεε.)
*Chrift, the brightnefs of his
(God's) glory, and the exprefs
image of his perfon.*

2 Cor. iv. 4.   Ὁς (Χριςος) εςιν εικων τε Θεε.
Chrift, who is the Image of God.

V.

Superiour to the angels.   Ὑπερανω τετων
(Αγγελων) Λογος Θειος.[1]

———

Heb. i. 4.   Κρειττων γενομενος των Αγγελων.
Chrift made fuperiour to Angels.

Heb. i. 6.   Και προσκυνησατωσαν αυτω παντες
Αγγελοι Θεε.
*Let all the Angels of God wor-
fhip him.*

VI. Su-

[1] De Profugis, V. i. p. 561. l. 15.

VI.

Superiour to all things in the world. ʻο Λογος τε Θεε ὑπερανω παντος ες τε Κοσμε.[1]

Heb. ii. 8. Παντα ὑπεταξας (ὁ Θεος) ὑποκατω των ποδων αυτε.

Thou haft put all things in fub-jeɛtion under his feet.

VII.

The Inftrument, by whom the world was made. ʻΟ Λογος αυτε, ᾧ καθαπερ οργανω προσ-χρησαμενος (ὁ Θεος) εκοσμοποιει.[2]

It was the divine Word, by whom all things were ordered and difpofed — Τον Θειον Λογον τον ταυτα διακοσμησαντα.

John i. 3. Παντα δι' αυτε (τε Λογε) εγενετο, και χωρις αυτε εγενετο εδε ἑν, ὁ γεγονεν.

All things were made by him, (the Logos) and without him was not any thing made, that was made.

1 Cor.

[1] De Leg. Allegor. V. i. p. 121. l. 44.

[2] Ib. V. i. p. 106. l. 29. p. 162. l. 15. p. 656. l. 50.

[3] De Mundi Opificio, V. i. p. 4. l. 43.

1 Cor. viii. 6. Ιησες Χριςος, δι' ε τα παντα.
*Jesus Christ, by whom are all
things.*

Heb. i. 2. Ὁν εθηκε Θεος κληρονομον παντων,
δι' ε και τες αιωνας εποιησεν.
Christ the Son of God—*whom
he hath appointed heir of all
things: by whom also he made
the worlds.*

Heb. i. 10. Εργα των χειρων σε ειτιν οι Ουρανοι.
*The Heavens are the work of
thy hands.*

VIII.

The great Substitute of God—Ὑπαρχος
τε Θεε—upon whom all things depend.[1]
Την αταξιαν και ακοσμιαν εις ταξιν και κοσμον
αγαγων, και το παν ὑπερεισας, ινα ςηριχθη
βεβαιως τω κραταιω και Ὑπαρχω με Λογω[2]—
*I am the God, who, having reduced all things
from disorder and irregularity to harmony and
beauty, fixed them upon a sure basis, and established
them under my all-powerful Word, the Logos.*

Ephes.

[1] De Agricult. V. i. p. 308. l. 30.
[2] De Somniis. V. i. p. 656. l. 48.

Ephes. iii. 9. Θεω τω τα παντα κτισαντι δια
Ιησ8 Χρις8.

God—who created all things by
Jesus Christ.

Phil. ii. 7. Μορφην δελ8 λαϐων.

Who took upon him the form of
a servant:

John xvii. 4. Το εργον ετελειωσα, ὁ δεδωκας μοι,
ἱνα ποιησω.

I have finished the work, which
thou gavest me to do.

John i. 3. Χωρις αυτ8 εγενετο 8δε ἑν.

Without him was not any thing
made, that was made.

IX.

The Light of the world, and intellectual
Sun. Ὁ Λογος φως —Ἡλιος νοητος.[1]

———————

John i. 9. Ὁ Λογος . . . . το φως το αληθινον.

The Word ... was the true light.

John i. 4. Το φως των ανθρωπων.

The life and light of men.

1 Pet.

[1] De Somniis, V. i. p. 6. 414. 632, 633.

H

1 Pet. ii. 9.   Χριϛɤ, τɤ εκ σκοτɤς ὑμας καλεσαντος εις το Θαυμαϛον αυτɤ φως.
*Chrift, who hath called you out
of darknefs into his marvellous
light.*

John viii. 12.   Εγω ειμι το φως τɤ κοσμɤ· ὁ ακο-
λɤθων εμοι ɤ μη περιπατησει εν τη
σκοτια, αλλ᾽ ἑξει το φως της ζωης.
*I am the light of the world: he
that followeth me fhall not walk
in darknefs, but fhall have the
light of life.*

X.

The Logos only can fee God.   Ὡ μονῳ
τον Θεον εξεϛι καθοραν.[1]

–––––––––––

John vi. 46.   Ὁ ων παρα τɤ Θεɤ, ɤτος ἑωρακε
τον Πατερα.
He that is of God (the Logos),
he hath feen the Father.

John

[1] De Confufione Linguar, V. i. p. 418 l. 39.

John i. 18. Θεον ϗδεις εωρακε ϖωποτε. Ὁ μονογενης Ὑιος, ὁ ων εις τον κολπον
τϗ Πατρος, εκεινος εξηγησατο.

*No man hath feen God at any
time. The only begotten Son,
which is in the bofom of the
Father, he hath declared him.*

XI.

He has God for his portion and refides
in him. Ὁ Λογος . . . . αυτον τον Θεον κληρον
εχων, εν αυτω μονω κατοικησει.[1]

John xiv. 11. Εγω (ειμι) εν τω Πατρι, και ὁ
Πατηρ εν εμοι.

*I am in the Father, and the
Father is in me.*

John i. 1. Εν αρχη ην ὁ Λογος, και ὁ Λογος
ην ϖρος τον Θεον.

*In the beginning was the Word,
and the Word was with God.*

John i. 18. Ὁ ων εις τον κολπον τϗ Πατρος.

*The Logos, or Word, which is
in the bofom of the Father.*

XII. He

[1] De Prof. V. i. p. 561. l. 27.

XII.

He is the moſt ancient of God's works.
Τον Αγγελον τον πρεσβυτατον.[1]

And was before all things. Πρεσβυτατος
των ὁσα γεγονε.[2]

John xvii. 5. Νυν δοξασον με συ, Πατερ, παρα
σεαυτῳ τῃ δοξῃ, ῃ ειχον προ τε
τον Κοσμον ειναι, παρα σοι.
*Now, O Father, glorify thou
me with thine own ſelf, with
the glory, which I had with
thee, before the world was.*

John i. 2. Ὁυτος ην εν αρχη προς τον Θεον.
*He was in the beginning with
God.*

2 Tim. i. 9. προ χρονων αιωνιων.
before all worlds.

John

[1] De Confuſ. Ling. Vol. i. p. 427. l. 3.

[2] De Leg. Alleger V. i. p. 121. l. 45. See alſo p. 562.

John xvii. 24. ηγαπησας με προ καταβολης κοσμε.

O Father, thou lovedst me before the foundation of the world.

Heb. i. 2. δι' ε και τες αιωνας εποιησεν.

By Whom (the Logos) *he made the worlds.*

XIII.

The Logos esteemed the same as God.

Λογον, ὡς αυτον (Θεον) κατανοεσι. [1]

Rom. ix. 5. Ὁ ων επι παντων Θεος ευλογητος εις τες αιωνας.

Christ — who is over all, God blessed for ever.

Mark ii. 7. Τις δυναται αφιεναι ἁμαρτιας, ει μη ἑις ὁ Θεος ;

Who can forgive sins, but God only?

Phil. ii. 6. Ὁς εν μορφη Θεε ὑπαρχων, εχ ἁρπαγμον ἡγησατο το ειναι ισα Θεῳ.

Who, being in the form of God, thought it no robbery to be equal with God.

XIV. The

[1] De Somniis, V. i. p. 656. l. 37.

XIV.

The Logos eternal — Ὁ αἰδιος Λογος. [1]

John xii. 34. Χριςος μενει εις τον αιωνα.

Chriſt abideth for ever.

2 Tim. i. 9. — προ χρονων αιωνιων.

Who was — *before the world began.*

2 Tim. iv. 18. ᾧ ἡ δοξα εις τꙋς αιωνας των αιωνων.

To whom be glory for ever and ever.

Heb. i. 8. Προς δε τον Ὑιον (λεγει,) Ὁ θρονος σꙋ, ὁ Θεος, εις τον αιωνα τꙋ αιωνος.

But to the Son he ſaith — Thy throne, O God, is for ever and ever.

Apoc. x. 6. Και ωμοσεν εν τῳ ζωντι εις τꙋς αιωνας των αιωνων, ὁς εκτισε τον ουρανον. . . . και την γην.

And he ſware by him, that liveth for ever and ever, who created heaven . . . and the earth.

XV. He

[1] De Plant. Noæ. V. i. p. 332. l. 32. Alſo V. ii. p. 604.

XV.

He fees all things. Οξυδερκεςατος, ὡς παν]α
εφοραν ειναι ἱκανος. [1]

Heb. iv. 12. Ζων γαρ ὁ Λογος τʊ Θεʊ, και
ενεργης . . . .

13. Και ʊκ εςι κτισις αφανης ενωπιον
αυτʊ (τʊ Λογʊ)· Παντα δε γυμνα
και τετραχηλισμενα τοις οφθαλμοις
αυτʊ, κ. τ. λ.

For the Word of God is quick
and powerful . . .
Neither is there any thing created, that is not manifeſt in his
fight : but all things are naked
and open to the eyes of him, &c.

Apoc. ii. 23. Εγω ειμι ὁ ερευνων νεφρʊς και
καρδιας.

I am he, who fearcheth the reins
and hearts.

XVI. He

[1] De Leg. Alleg. V. i. p. 121. l. 3.

XVI.

He supports the World. Ὁ τε γαρ τε Οντος Λογος, δεσμος ων των ἁπαντων. . . . . . συνεχει τα μερη παντα, και σφιγγει [1] — *The Logos is the connecting power, by which all things are united. . . . . . He makes all the various parts of the universe unite, and he preserves them in that union.*

Ὁ θειος Λογος περιεχει τα ὁλα, και πεπληρωκεν.[2] *The divine Word surrounds and upholds all things, and has brought them to perfection.*

John iii. 35. Ὁ Πατηρ. . . . παντα δεδωκεν εν τη χειρι αυτε.

The Father hath given all things into his hands.

Heb. i. 3. φερων τε τα παντα τω ρηματι της δυναμεως αυτε.

Upholding all things by the Word of his power.

Coloss. i. 17. τα παντα εν αυτω συνεςηκε.

By him all things consist.

XVII. The

[1] De Prof. V. i. p. 562. l. 34.

[2] Frag. V. ii. p. 655. l. 35.   Also V. i. p. 330. p 499. V. ii. p. 604, 606.

XVII.

The Logos neareſt to God without any ſeparation; being as it were fixed and founded upon the only true exiſting Deity, nothing coming between to diſturb that unity. Ὁ Λογος Θειος. . . . των νοητων ἁπαξ-απαντων ὁ πρεσϐυτατος, ὁ εγγυτατω, μηδενος οντος μεθοριᾳ διαςηματος, τᵹ μονᵹ, ὁ εςιν αψευδως, αφιδρυμενος. [1]

John x. 30. Εγω και ὁ Πατηρ ἑν εσμεν.

I and my Father are one.

John xvii. 11. Πατερ ἁγιε, τηρησον αυτᵹς. . . ἱνα ωσιν ἑν, καθως ἡμεις.

Holy Father, keep thoſe, whom thou haſt given me: that they may be one, as we are.

John xiv. 11. Εγω εν τῳ Πατρι, και ὁ Πατηρ εν εμοι.

I am in the Father, and the Father in me.

John i. 18. Ὁ μονογενης υἱος, ὁ ων εις τον κολπον τᵹ Πατρος.

The only begotten Son, who is in the boſom of the Father.

XVIII. The

[1] De Profugis, V. i. p. 561. l. 15.

XVIII.

The Logos free from all taint of fin, either voluntary or involuntary. Ὁ μεν (Λογος) ανευ τροπης εκυσιυ .... και της ακυσιυ.[1]

Heb. ix. 14. Ἁιμα τυ Χριςυ, ὁς ..... ἑαυτον προσηνεγκεν αμωμον τω Θεω.
The blood of Chrift, who .... offered himself without fpot to God.

John viii. 46. Τις εξ ὑμων ελεγχει με περι ἁμαρτιας;
Which of you convinceth me of fin?

1 Pet. ii. 22. Χριςος, ...ὁς ἁμαρτιαν υκ εποιησεν, υδε ἑυρεθη δολος εν τω ςοματι αυτυ.
Who did no fin, neither was guile found in his mouth.

XIX. Of

---

[1] De Profugis, V. i. p. 561. l. 25.

XIX.

Of the Logos prefiding over the imperfect, and God only over the perfect and wife.

Ὁυτος γαρ (ὁ Λογος) ἡμων των ατελων αν ειη Θεος, των δε σοφων και τελειων ὁ Πρωτος — *For the Logos may be efteemed the God of us, who are imperfect: but of the wife and perfect, Firft and Chief muft be looked upon as the God.* [1]

Philo was not confiftent, when he made this difference; and did not confider, that God's mercy is not limited, but " is over all his works." Befides, in refpect to the Logos, he confeffes, as will be prefently feen, that he diftributes his heavenly affiftance equally to all, who feek it. And fo far from his goodnefs being confined to the imperfect only, Philo has juft before faid— τρεφεται δε των μεν τελειοτερων ἡ ψυχη ὁλῳ τῳ Λογῳ —*The foul of the more pure is nourifhed by the full influence of the Word or Logos.* [2]

He

---

[1] De Leg. Allegor. V. i. p. 128. l. 43.

[2] Ibid. p. 122. l. 6.

He was probably led to form this judgment, concerning the weak and fimple being folely delegated to the Logos, from the Chriftian doctrines, with which he had gained acquaintance, and which he did not perfectly underftand. The Logos in the character of Chrift did extend his faving help peculiarly to thofe, who were in a ftate of fpiritual debility, but not exclufively of others.

Matth. xi. 5. — πτωχοι ευαγγελιζονται.
The poor have the Gofpel preached unto them.

Luke v. 32. Ουκ εληλυθα καλεσαι δικαιυς, αλλ' αμαρτωλυς εις μετανοιαν.
I came not to call the righteous, but finners to repentance.

1 Tim. i. 15. Πιςος ο Λογος . . . οτι Χριςος Ιησυς ηλθεν εις τον κοσμον αμαρτωλυς σωσαι.
This is a faithful faying . . . that Chrift Jefus came into the world to fave finners.

XX. The

XX.

The Logos is the fountain of wisdom; to which all should most diligently repair, that, by drinking from that sacred Spring, they may instead of death obtain everlasting life. Προτρεπει δε κν τον μεν ωκυδρομειν ἱκανον, συντεινειν απνευςι προς τον ανωτατω Λογον Θειον, ὁς σοφιας ες πηγη, ἱνα αρυσαμενος τκ ναματος, αντι Θανατκ Ζωην Αϊδιον αθλον εὑρηται. *It is of the greatest consequence to every person, that can make his way in the course, which is set before him, to strive without remission to approach to the divine Logos, the Word of God above, who is the fountain of all wisdom ; that, by drinking largely of that sacred Spring, instead of death he may be hereafter rewarded with everlasting life.*[1] This I quote at large, it being so very remarkable. Ρημα Θεκ και Λογον Θειον, αφ' κ τασαι παιδειαι και σοφιαι ῥεκσιν αενναοι.[2]

1 Cor.

---

[1] De Profugis. V. i. p. 560. l. 31.

[2] Ibid. p. 566. l. 9.

1 Cor. i. 24. Χριςον Θεε δυναμιν και Θεε σοφιαν. *Chriſt the power of God and the wiſdom of God.*

Coloſſ. ii. 3. εν ᾡ εισι παντες οἱ Θησαυροι της σοφιας. *In whom are hid all the treaſures of wiſdom and knowledge.*

John iv. 14. Ὁς δ'αν πιη εκ τε ὑδατος, ἑ εγω δωσω αυτω, ἐ μη διψηση εις τον αιωνα. αλλα το ὑδωρ, ὁ δωσω αυτω, γενησεται εν αυτω πηγη ὑδατος αλλομενε εις Ζωην Αιωνιον. *Whoſoever drinketh of the water, that I ſhall give him, ſhall never thirſt : but the water, that I ſhall give him, ſhall be in him a well of water ſpringing up into ever- laſting life.*

John vii. 38. Ὁ πιςευων εις εμε . . . . . ποταμοι εκ της κοιλιας αυτε ῥευσεσιν ὑδατος ζωντος. *He that believeth in me — out of his belly ſhall flow rivers of living waters.*

XXI. The

XXI.

The Logos is a Meſſenger ſent by God to man, his liege ſubject. Πρεσβευτης τυ ἡγεμονος προς το ὑπκοον.

———

John viii. 42.   Ου γαρ απ᾽εμαυτυ εληλυθα, αλλ᾽ εκεινος (ὁ Θεος) με απεςειλε.
I came not of myſelf, but he (God) ſent me.

John v. 36.   Ὁ Πατηρ με απεςαλκε.
The Father hath ſent me.

1 John iv. 9.   Τον υἱον αυτυ .... απεςαλκεν ὁ Θεος εις τον κοσμον, ἱνα ζησωμεν δι᾽αυτυ.
God ſent his only begotten Son into the world, that we might live through him.

John viii. 29.   Και ὁ πεμψας με μετ᾽ εμυ εςιν.
And he, that ſent me, is with me.

XXII. He

¹ Quis Rer. Div. Hæres. Vol. 1. p. 501. l. 49.

XXII.

He is the Advocate, and Interceſſor for
mortal man. Ὁ δ᾽ αυτος (ὁ Λογος) ἱκετης μεν
ἐςι τȣ θνητȣ.[1]

John xiv. 16. Εγω ερωτησω τον Πατερα, και
αλλον Παρακλητον δωσει ὑμιν.
*I will pray the Father, and he
ſhall give you another Comforter.*

John xvii. 20. Ου ϖερι τȣτων δε ερωτω μονον,
αλλα και ϖερι των ϖιςευσοντων
δια τȣ λογȣ αυτων εις εμε.
*Neither pray I for theſe alone;
but for them alſo, which ſhall believe on me through their word.*

Heb. vii. 25. Παντοτε ζων εις το εντυγχανειν
ὑπερ αυτων.
Chriſt — *ever living to make
interceſſion for them.*

Rom. viii. 34. Ὁς και εςιν εν δεξια τȣ Θεȣ, ὁς
και εντυγχανει ὑπερ ἡμων.
*Who is even at the right hand
of God, who alſo maketh interceſſion for us.*

XXIII. He

XXIII.

He ordered and difpofed all things. 'ο τε
γαρ Θειος Λογος τα εν τη φυσει διειλε και διενειμε
παντα. *The divine Logos feparated, and re-
gulated all things in the world.*[1]

Τομευς ἁπαντων ὁ Ἱερος και Θειος Λογος. *The
facred and divine Logos was the Perfon, that
diftributed and appointed all things.*[2]

———————————————

Heb. xi. 3.   Νοεμεν κατηρτισθαι τες αιωνας
ῥηματι Θεε.
*We underftand, that the worlds
were framed by the Word of
God.*

Coloff.

[1] Quis Rer. Divin. Hæres. V. i. p. 506. l. 10.

[2] Ibid. p. 504. l. 31.

I

Coloſſ. i. 15, 16. Χριϛος . . . . . πρωτοτοκος πασης
κτισεως, οτι εν αυτω εκτισθη τα
παντα, τα εν τοις ϱρανοις, και
τα επι της γης, τα ὁρατα, και
τα αορατα . . . . τα παντα δι᾽
αυτϧ, και εις αυτον, εκτιϛαι.

*Chriſt . . . the firſt-born of every
creature. For by him were all
things created, that are in heaven, and that are in earth, viſible
and inviſible . . . All things were
created by him and for him.*

XXIV.

He is the Shepherd of God's flock.
Ὡς ποιμην και βασιλευς ὁ Θεος αγει (παντα)
κατα δικην και νομον, προϛησαμενος τον ορθον αυτϧ
Λογον, πρωτογονον υἱον, ὁς την επιμελειαν της ἱερας
ταυτης αγελης, ὁια τις μεγαλϧ βασιλεως Ὑπαρχος,
διαδεξεται. *The Deity, like a ſhepherd, and at
the ſame time a monarch, aɛts with the moſt con-
ſummate order and reɛtitude; and has appointed
his Firſt-born, the upright Logos, like the
Subſtitute of a mighty prince, to take the care
of his ſacred flock.*[1]

Heb.

Heb. xiii. 20. Ποιμενα των προβατων τον μεγαν
.... τον Κυριον ἡμων Ιησυν.

*The great Shepherd of the flock
...our Lord Jesus.*

John x. 14. Εγω ειμι ὁ ποιμην ὁ καλος, και
γινωσκω τα εμα, και γινωσκομαι
ὑπο των εμων.

*I am the good Shepherd, and
know my sheep, and am known
of mine.*

1 Pet. ii. 25. Χριςον ... τον ποιμενα και επισκοπον των ψυχων ὑμων.

*Christ .... the Shepherd, and
Guardian of your souls.*

XXV.

Of the Power and Royalty of the Logos,
as described by Philo, who mentions him as
*The great Governour of the world, and speaks
of his creative and princely power: for through
them the heavens and the whole world were produced.* Ὁ τε Ἡγεμονος Λογος, και ἡ ποιητικη
και βασιλικη δυναμις αυτυ. Τυτων γαρ ὁ τε
Ουρανος, και συμπας ὁ κοσμος.[1]

1 Cor.

[1] De Profugis, V. i. p. 561. l. 33.

1 Cor. xv. 25. Δει γαρ αυτον (Χριςον) βασιλευειν αχρις ὑ αν 9η παντας τυς εχθρυς ὑπο τυς ποδας αυτυ.

For Chrift muſt reign till he hath put all his enemies under his feet.

Eph. i. 21, 22. Χριςος .... ὑπερανω πασης αρχης και εξυσιας και δυναμεως και κυριοτητος και παντος ονοματος ονομαζομενυ, υ μονον εν τω αιωνι τυτω, αλλα και εν τω μελλοντι· και παντα (ὁ Θεος) ὑπεταξεν ὑπο τυς ποδας αυτυ.

Chrift ... above all principality, and might, and dominion, and every name, that is named, not only in this world but in the world to come ... and God hath put all things under his feet.

Heb. i. 2, 3. Δι᾽ ὑ και (ὁ Θεος) τυς αιωνας εποιησεν.

By whom alſo God made the worlds.

Apoc. xvii. 14. Ὁτι κυριος κυριων εςι, και βασι- λευς βασιλεων.

For he is Lord of lords, and King of kings.

‚ l. The

XXVI.

The Logos the Phyſician that heals all evil.

Τον Αγγελον (ὁς ἐςι Λογος) ὡσπερ Ιατρον κακων.

Luke iv. 18. Πνευμα Κυριε ἐπ' ἐμε ... ιασασθαι
τες συντετριμμενες την καρδιαν.
*The Spirit of the Lord is upon
me, becauſe he hath anointed me
. . . . to heal the broken-hearted.*

1 Pet. ii. 24. Τῳ μωλωπι αυτε ιαθητε.
By whoſe ſtripes ye were healed.

Luke vii. 21. Εν αυτη δε τη ὡρα εθεραπευσε
πολλες απο νοσων και μαςιγων,
και πνευματων πονηρων.
*In that ſame hour he cured
many of their infirmities, and
plagues, and of evil ſpirits.*

James i. 21. Δεξασθε τον εμφυτον λογον, τον
δυναμενον σωσαι τας ψυχας ὑμων.
*Receive with meekneſs the en-
grafted word, which is able to
ſave your ſouls.*

XXVII. The

De Leg. Allegor. V. i. p. 122. l. 17.

I 3

XXVII.

The Seal of God. Ὁ δὲ τε ποιενντος (τον Κοσμον) Λογος αυτος εςιν ἡ σφραγις, ἡ των οντων ἑκαςον μεμορφωται . . . . ἀτε εκμαγειον και εικων τελειε Λογε. *The Logos, by whom the world was framed, is the Seal, after the impreſſion of which every thing is made . . . and is rendered the ſimilitude, and image of the perfect Word of God.*[1]

Ανθρωπε ψυχην . . . . . τυπωθεισαν σφραγιδι . . . ἡς ὁ χαρακτηρ εςιν αιδιος Λογος. *The ſoul of man is an impreſſion of a Seal, of which the proto-type, and original characteriſtick, is the everlaſting Logos.*[2]

John vi. 27.   Τετον γαρ (Ιησεν) ὁ Πατηρ εσφραγισεν.
Jeſus, the Son of man . . . him hath the Father ſealed.

Epheſ.

[1] De Profugis, V. i. p. 547. l. 49. p. 548. l. 2.

Ephef. i. 13. Εσφραγισθητε τω πνευματι της επαγγελιας τω ἁγιω.

In whom alfo, after that ye believed, ye were fealed with that holy Spirit of promife.

Heb. i. 3. Χριςος . . . απαυγασμα . . . . . και χαρακτηρ της ὑποςασεως αυτε (τε Θεε.)

Chrift, the brightnefs of his (God's) *glory, and the exprefs image of his perfon.*

XXVIII.

The Logos the fure refuge, to whom before all others we ought to feek. Ὁ Θειος Λογος, εφ᾽ ὁν πρωτον καταφευγειν ωφελιμωτατον.[r]

Matt. xi. 28. Δευτε προς με παντες ὁι κοπιωντες και πεφορτισμενοι, καγω αναπαυσω ὑμας.

Come to me, all ye, that labour, and are heavy laden, and I will give you reft.

1 Peter

[r] De Profugis, V. i. p. 560. l. 14.

I 4

1 Peter ii. 25. Ητε γαρ ως προβατα πλανωμενα·
αλλ᾿ επεςραφητε νυν επι τον ποι-
μενα και επισκοπον των ψυχων
ὑμων.

*Ye were as sheep going astray,
but are now returned unto the
Shepherd, and the guardian of
your souls.*

XXIX.

Of spiritual food — την ϵρανιον τροφην ψυχης
— *the heavenly nutriment of the soul*, equally
distributed by the Logos to all, who want it,
and will make a good use of it.[1]

Mark xiii. 10. Εις παντα τα εθνη δει κηρυχθηναι
το Ευαʳγελιον.

*The Gospel must be published
among all nations.*

Matt. xxiv. 14. Και κηρυχθησεται τετο το ευαγ-
γελιον . . . . εν ὁλη τη οικεμενη.

*And this Gospel of the kingdom
shall be preached in all the
world.*

Mat.

[1] Quis Rerum. Divin. Hæres. V. i. p. 499. l. 44.

Mat. xxviii. 19. Μαθητευσατε παντα τα εθνη.

Go ye therefore, and teach all nations.

John iii. 17. Ου γαρ απεςειλεν ὁ Θεος τον υἱον αυτȣ εις τον κοσμον, ἱνα κρινη τον κοσμον, αλλ᾽ ἱνα σωθη ὁ κοσμος δι᾽ αυτȣ.

God sent not his Son into the world to condemn the world, but that the world through him might be saved.

Rom. x. 18. —εις πασαν την γην εξηλθεν ὁ φθοΓγος αυτων, και εις τα περατα της οικȣμενης τα ῥηματα αυτων.

Their sound went into all the earth, and their words to the ends of the world.

Matt. vii. 7. Ζητειτε, και ἑυρησετε· κρȣετε, και ανοιγησεται ὑμιν.

Seek, and ye shall find; knock, and it shall be opened unto you.

Matt. v. 6.

Μακαριοι οι πεινωντες και διψωντες την δικαιοσυνην, οτι αυτοι χορτασθησονται.

Bleſſed are they, which do hunger and thirſt after righteouſneſs; for they ſhall be filled.

Rom. x. 12.

Ὁ γαρ αυτος Κυριος παντων πλυτων εις παντας τυς επικαλυμενυς αυτον.

The ſame Lord, who is over all, is rich unto all, that call upon him.

XXX.

ΕΛΕΥΘΕΡΙΑ.

Of men's forſaking their ſins, and returning to their duty: by which they obtain ελευθερια της ψυχης—*freedom of the ſoul.* [1]

Alſo of their being brought from a ſtate of vaſſalage, and exile, to ſpiritual liberty by the Logos. [2]

2 Cor.

[1] De C. Q. Erud. Gratiâ. V. i. p. 534. l. 44.

[2] De Profugis. V. i. p. 561. l. 33. p. 563. l. 25.

2 Cor. iii. 17. Ὁ δε Κυριος το πνευμα εϛιν. ἐ δε
το πνευμα Κυριϰ, εϰει ελευθερια.

*Now the Lord is that spirit:
and where the spirit of the Lord
is, there is liberty.*

Galat. v. 1. Τη ελευθερια ϰν, ἡ Χριϛος ἡμας
ηλευθερωσε, ϛηϰετε.

*Stand fast therefore in the
liberty, wherewith Christ hath
made us free.*

Galat. v. 13. Ὑμεις γαρ επ' ελευθερια εϰληθητε.

*For, brethren, ye have been
called unto liberty.*

1 Cor. vii. 22. Ὁ γαρ εν Κυριῳ ϰληθεις δϰλος
απελευθερος Κυριϰ εϛιν.

*For he that is called in the
Lord, being a servant, is the
Lord's freeman.*

John viii. 36. Εαν ϰν ὁ Ὑιος ὑμας ελευθερωση,
οντως ελευθεροι εσεσθε.

*If the Son therefore shall make
you free, ye are free indeed.*

XXXI. The

XXXI.

The happy confequences of men's beft endeavours. They are by the fame Logos freed from all corruption, and entitled to immortality hereafter. Τοτε γαρ αυτην (την ψυχην) των αθλων αγαμενος ὁ ῾Ιερος Λογος ετιμησε, γερας εξαιρετον δες, κληρον αθανατον, την εν αφ-θαρτω γενει ταξιν.[1]

---

1 Cor. xv. 52. ῾Οι νεκροι (εν Χριςω) εγερθησονται αφθαρτοι.

The dead (in Chrift) fhall be raifed incorruptible.

1 Cor. xv. 53. Δει γαρ το φθαρτον τετο ενδυ-σασθαι αφθαρσιαν.

For this mortal muft put on immortality.

Rom. viii. 21. ῾Οτι και αυτη ἡ κτισις ελευθερω-θησεται απο της δελειας της φθορας εις την ελευθεριαν της δοξης των τεκνων τε Θεε.

Becaufe the creature itfelf alfo fhall be delivered from the bondage of corruption into the glorious liberty of the children of God.

1 Peter

1 Peter i. 3, 4. Ευλογητος ὁ Θεος . . . ὁ κατα το πολυ αυτ꞊ ελεος αναγεννησας ἡμας εις ελπιδα ζωσαν δι᾽ ανας꞊ασεως Ιησ꞊ Χρις꞊ εκ νεκρων, εις κληρονομιαν αφθαρτον, και αμιαντον, και αμαραντον, τετηρημενην εν Ουρανοις εις ἡμας.

Bleſſed be God . . . who, according to his abundant mercy, hath begotten us again unto a lively hope, by the reſurrection of Jeſus Chriſt from the dead; to an inheritance incorruptible, and undefiled, and that fadeth not away, reſerved in heaven for us.

XXXII.

Philo ſpeaks of the Logos, not only as the Son of God, and his firſt begotten; but alſo ſtyles him—αγαπητον τεκνον—*his beloved Son.*[1]

Matt. iii. 17. ῾Ουτος ες꞊ιν ὁ υἱος μ꞊ ὁ αγαπητος.
This is my beloved Son.

Luke

[1] De Leg. Alleg. V. i. p. 129. [1] 4.

Luke ix. 35.   Φωνη εγενετο εκ της νεφελης
λεγεσα, ὑτος εϛιν ὁ υἱος μϰ ὁ
αγαπητος, αυτϰ ακϰετε.

And there came a voice out of
the cloud, faying, This is my
beloved Son, hear him.

2 Pet. i. 17.   Ὁυτος εϛιν ὁ υἱος μϰ ὁ αγαπητος,
εις ὁν εγω ευδοκησα.

This is my beloved Son, in
whom I am well pleafed.

Coloff. i. 13.   Ὁ Ὑιος της αγαπης αυτϰ.

The Son of his love.

XXXIII.

He afks, by what means a man may
arrive at pure incorporeal happinefs; or as
he exprefles it — γενεσθαι των ασωματων και
θειων πραγματων κληρονομος — and anfwers —
Ὁ καταπνευσθεις ανωθεν — ὁ καθαρωτατος νϰς —
ὁ λυθεις των δεσμων, και ελευθερωθεις [1] —*He, who*
is infpired from above — who hath the pureft
mind — who is loofened from the fetters of this
world, and hath gained his fpiritual freedom —
he only can partake of this happinefs.

Matth.

[1] Quis R . . . . II . . . V . . p. 482 . . - 30.

Matth. v. 8. Μακαριοι ἱ καθαροι τη καρδια,
ὁτι αυτοι τον Θεον οψονται.

*lessed are the pure in heart,
for they shall see God.*

Rom. viii. 2. Ὁ γαρ νομος τȣ πνευματος της
ζωης εν Χριϛω Ιησȣ ηλευθερωσε με
απο τȣ νομȣ της ἁμαρτιας και
τȣ θανατȣ.

*For the law of the spirit of life
in Christ Jesus hath made me
free from the law of sin and
death.*

2 Pet. i. 4. Τα μεγιϛα ἡμιν και τιμια επαγ-
γελματα δεδωρηται, ινα δια τȣ-
των γενησθε θειας κοινωνοι φυσεως.

*Wherefore are given to us
exceeding great, and precious
promises; that by these ye may be
partakers of the divine nature.*

1 Cor. xiv. 1. Διωκετε την αγαπην, ζηλȣτε δε
τα πνευματικα.

*Follow after charity, and desire
spiritual gifts.*

Ibid. 12. Ζηλωται εϛε πνευματων (five
ασωματων.)

Ye seek after, what is spiritual,

XXXIV.

Of good Men admitted to the assembly of Saints above. Ὁι δε ανθρωπων μεν ὑφηγησεις απολελοιποτες, μαθηται δε Θεȣ ευφυεις γεγονοτες .... εις το αφθαρτον και τελεωτατον γενος μετανιϛανται. *Those, who relinquish human doctrines, and become the well disposed disciples of God, will be one day translated to an incorruptible, and perfect, order of beings.[1]*

Heb. xii. 22, 23. Αλλα προσεληλυθατε Σιων ορει, και πολει Θεȣ ζωντος .... και μυριασιν Αˠγελων . . . και πνευμασι δικαιων τετελειωμενων.

But ye are come unto mount Sion, and to the city of the living God, and to an innumerable company of angels, and to the spirits of just men made perfect.

Coloss.

Coloſſ. i. 12. Ευχαριςυντες τω πατρι, τω ίκα-
νωσαντι ήμας εις την μεριδα τυ
κληρυ των άγιων εν τω φωτι.
*Giving thanks unto the Father,
which hath made us meet to be
partakers of the inheritance of
Saints in light.*

XXXV.

Of the juſt Man not being given over to
utter death, but raiſed by the Word of God.
For through the Logos, by whom all things
were created, God will advance him to be
near himſelf in heaven.

Ήνικα γυν τελευταν εμελλεν, υκ εκλειπων
προςιθεται, ώσπερ οι προτεροι... αλλα δια ρηματος
τυ αιτιυ μετανιςαται, δι' ύ και ο συμπας κοσμος
εδημιυργειτο — Τω αυτω Λογω και το παν εργα-
ζομενος, και τον τελειον απο των περιγειων αναγων
ώς έαυτον[1] — ίδρυσας πλησιον έαυτυ.

For

[1] De Sacrificiis, V. i. p. 165. l. 7.   [2] Ibid. l. 5.

K

For when he is confrom. *he* *does not fail, nor is he added to the numbers, who have gone before him: but he is tranflated to another ftate by the Word of that great Caufe of all things, (the Logos), by whom the world was created — For God, by his faid Word, by. which he made all things, will raife the perfect man from the dregs of this world, and exalt him near himfelf: he will place him near his own perfon.*

John vi. 44. Ουδεις δυναται ελθειν προς με, εαν μη ὁ Πατηρ ὁ πεμψας με ἑλκυση αυτον· και εγω αναςησω αυτον τη εσχατη ἡμερα.

No man can come to me, except the Father, which hath fent me, draw him: and I will raife him up at the laft day.

John vi. 37. Παν, ὁ διδωσι μοι ὁ Πατηρ, προς εμε ἡξει.

All, that the Father giveth me, fhall come to me.

John

John xiv. 6. Ουδεις ερχεται προς τον Πατερα, ει μη δι' εμε.

No man cometh to the Father, but by me.

John xii. 26. Ὁπε ειμι εγω, εκει και ὁ διακονος ὁ εμος εςαι . . . . . και τιμησει αυτον ὁ Πατηρ.

Where I am, there alſo ſhall my ſervant be ... him will my Father honour.

XXXVI.

ΛΟΓΟΣ ΑΡΧΙΕΡΕΥΣ.

Of the Logos being the true High Prieſt; of his being without ſin, and anointed with oil. Ὁ κοσμος, εν ᾧ και Αρχιερευς, ὁ πρωτογονος αυτε Θειος Λογος.[1]——Λεγομεν γαρ τον Αρχιερεα εκ ανθρωπον, αλλα Λογον Θειον ειναι, παντων εχ ἑκεσιων μονον, αλλα και ακεσιων αδικηματων αμετοχον

[1] De Somniis, V. i. p. 653. l. 23.

αμετοχον — διοτι την κεφαλην κεχρισαι ελαιω.[*]

It is the world, in which the Logos, God's First-born, that great High Priest, resides. And I assert, that this High Priest is no man, but the Holy Word of God: who is not capable of either voluntary, or involuntary sin — and hence his head is anointed with oil.

Heb. iv. 14. Εχοντες εν Αρχιερεα μεγαν, διεληλυθοτα τες ερανες, Ιησεν τον υιον τε Θεε, κρατωμεν της ομολογιας.

Seeing then, that we have a great High Priest, that is passed into the heavens, Jesus the Son of God, let us hold fast our profession.

1 Pet. ii. 22. Ὁς ἁμαρτιαν εκ εποιησεν, εδε ευρεθη δολος εν τω ςοματι αυτε.

Who did no sin, neither was guile found in his mouth.

John

---

[*] De Profugis, V. i. p. 562. l. 13. and 22.

John viii. 46. Τις εξ ὑμων ελεγχει με περι
ἁμαρτιας;

*Which of you convinceth me of
fin?*

Acts iv. 27. Τον ἁγιον παιδα σε Ιησεν, ὁν
εχρισας.

*Thy holy Child Jefus, whom
thou haft anointed.*

John i. 41. Ευρηκαμεν τον Μεσσιαν, ὁ εςι
μεθερμηνευομενον ὁ Χριςος.

*We have found the Meffias,
which is, being interpreted,
the Chrift.* (i. e. the anointed.)

Heb. vii. 26. Αρχιερευς, ὁσιος, ακακος, αμι-
αντος, κεχωρισμενος απο των
ἁμαρτωλων.

*For fuch an High Prieft be-
came us, who is holy, harmlefs,
undefiled, feparate from finners.*

XXXVII.

ΛΟΓΟΣ ΑΡΧΙΕΡΕΥΣ ΜΕΘΟΡΙΟΣ, OR THE LOGOS IN HIS MEDIATORIAL CAPACITY.

Philo mentions the Logos as the Great High Prieſt and Mediator for the ſins of the world.[1] And, ſpeaking of the rebellion of Korah, he introduces the Logos as ſaying — Κἀγω εἱϛηκειν ανα μεσον Κυριε και ὑμων.[2]—*It was I, who ſtood in the middle between the Lord and you.* For this province was delegated to him by God the Father — ἱνα μεθοριος ϛας το γενομενον διακρινῃ τϗ ϖεποιηκοτος[3] —*that by ſtanding as a mediator between both, he might ſeparate the creature from the Creator.* He had before ſaid — Θαυμαζω και τον μετα σϖϗδης απνευϛι δραμοντα συντονως Ἱερον Λογον, ἱνα ϛῃ μεσος των τεθνηκοτων και των ζωντων.—
I can-

[1] De Somniis, V. i. p. 653. l. 14.

[2] Quis Rerùm Divin. Hæres. V. i. p. 502. l. 1.

[3] Ibid. p. 501. l. 46.

I cannot without admiration view the sacred Logos, pressing with such zeal and without remission, that he may stand between the dead and the living.[1] The High Priest, who went once in a year into the Holy of Holies, was a type of one greater, who was to come. Philo describes this sacred apartment as — εσωτατω τε Ἱερε — αυτα τα αδυτα, εις ἁ ἁπαξ τε ενιαυτε ὁ Μεγας Ἱερευς εισερχεται, τη νηςεια λεγομενη, μονον επιθυμιασων, και κατα τα πατρια ευξομενος φοραν αγαθων, ευετηριαν τε και ειρηνην ἁπασιν ανθρωποις — *The very innermost recess of the temple — the holy Sanctuary, into which the High Priest once in a year upon the day of the fast entered, merely to offer up incense, and to make supplication after the rites of his country for the produce of all good things, and for plenty and peace to the whole world.*[2] In this account Philo must have been in some respects wilfully mistaken. He must have known, that the

office

---

[1] Quis Rer. Div. Hæres. Vol. i. p. 501. l. 19.

[2] De Virtutibus, V. ii. 591. l. 5.

office of the High Prieſt at this ſeaſon was to perform an act of atonement. It was *an everlaſting ſtatute to make atonement for the children of Iſrael for all their ſins once a year.*[1] As to any prayers to obtain — φοραν των αγαθων — *plenty or produce*, no ſuch were made; much leſs for the univerſal peace and happineſs of mankind. I do not believe, that the word *pray*, or *prayer*, is to be found in any one ordinance of Moſes. He therefore impoſed upon the emperour Caligula, when he made this declaration before him, What he ſays, of the Logos being the Interceſſor for man, a Mediator for Sin, is true : but it was the Logos in a capacity, which he could not be brought to allow. The whole is very truly deſcribed by St. Paul, who mentions Chriſt as both High Prieſt and Mediator — a High Prieſt, who has once for all entered the true Holy of Holies, Heaven; and makes interceſſion for us.

Heb.

---

[1] Lev. xvi. 34.

Heb. viii. 1--6. Εχομεν Αρχιερεα, ὁς εκαθισεν εν δεξια τε θρονε της μεγαλωσυνης εν τοις ερανοις, των ἁγιων λει- τεργος .... κρειτ]ονος διαθηκης μεσιτης.

We have such an High Priest, who is set on the right hand of the throne of the Majesty in the heavens; a Minister of the sanctuary ... a Mediator of a better covenant.

Heb. ix. 24. Ου γαρ εις χειροποιητα ἁγια εισηλθεν ὁ Χριςος, αντιτυπα των αληθινων, αλλ᾽ εις αυτον τον ερανον, νυν εμφανισθηναι τω προσωπω τε Θεε ὑπερ ἡμων.

For Christ is not entered into holy places made with hands, which were types of the true; but into heaven itself, now to appear in the presence of God for us.

Heb.

Heb. ix. 11, 12. Χριϛος δε παραγενομενος Αρχιερευς των μελλοντων αγαθων, δια
της μειζονος και τελειοτερας σκηνης, ȣ χειροποιητȣ, τȣτεϛιν, ȣ ταυτης της κτισεως, ȣδε δι᾽ αιματος
τραγων και μοσχων, δια δε τȣ ιδιȣ
αιματος εισηλθεν εφαπαξ εις τα
αγια, αιωνιον λυτρωσιν ευραμενος.

*But Chriſt being come an High
Prieſt of good things to come,
by a greater and more perfect
tabernacle, not made with
hands, that is to ſay, not of
this* (worldly) *building; neither by the blood of goats, and
calves, but by his own blood he
entered in once into the holy
place, having obtained eternal
redemption for us.*

1 Tim. ii. 5. Ἐις γαρ Θεος, ἑις και μεσιτης Θεȣ
και ανθρωπων, ανθρωπος Χριϛος
Ιησȣς.

*For there is one God, and one
Mediator between God and
man, the man Jeſus Chriſt.*

XXXVIII. Con-

XXXVIII.

Concerning the fix cities of refuge, to which people guilty of accidental homicide were to repair; and of their return from exile upon the death of the High Prieft.

And the Lord fpake unto Mofes. — Ye fhall give three cities on this fide Jordan, and three cities fhall ye give in the land of Canaan, which fhall be cities of refuge: — that every one, that killeth another unawares may flee thither. — And he fhall abide in it unto the death of the High Prieft, which was anointed with the holy oil.[1]

XXX.

Philo's opinion concerning thefe cities and the death of the High Prieft.

Though he in general fuppofes, that the ordinances concerning the Levites and the High Prieft were limited to them, and had no further meaning; and is of the fame opinion

[1] Numbers xxxv. 10. 14. 25.

opinion in refpect to the other folemn appointments; yet he is forced in fome inftances to allow, that there was fomething farther meant, and that the High Prieft mentioned was a type of one far greater: and he gives his reafons for his opinion. His words I have before quoted: but I fhall repeat the purport of them, as they deferve to be farther confidered.

He fays,[1] that he was for fometime in a ftate of doubt and perplexity concerning the nature of this ordinance, when he confidered it literally. For the punifhment did not feem to be equally impofed, as the perfons were alike guilty. Some muft have fled away at the commencement of the Priefthood; and others when the Prieft was near his diffolution. Hence, fome muft have been in a ftate of exile for years, and others poffibly for only a few days. He therefore concludes with faying, that the High Prieft ultimately alluded

---

[1] See p 91, 92, 93. of this Treatife.

alluded to was the divine [1] Logos: and the ftate of exile was his withdrawing his influence from the foul of man. [2] We fee that he came near the mark, but could not attain to it. In confequence of this he has brought himfelf into as great difficulties, as thofe, which he fought to avoid.

This great perfonage was certainly the Logos; but the Logos in his human capacity, Jefus Chrift the Meffiah; who was alluded to under the character of the High Prieft *anointed with oil*. He was to free the world from a ftate of exile, and fpiritual bondage; and procure liberty to the foul. This was effected by the death of the Meffiah, [3] the true High Prieft; a circumftance, which Philo could not comprehend. By his wrong application of the truth, he is obliged with much refinement to attribute this death to a perfon incapable of dying; and

---

[1] Λεγομεν γαρ τον Αρχιερεα εκ ανθρωπον, αλλα Λογον Θειον ειναι. V. i. p. 562. l. 13.

[2] De Profugis, V. i. p. 563. l. 24.

[3] 1 Cor. xv. 3. Απεθανεν υπερ των αμαρτιων ημων 2 Cor. v. 15. —

and in the end he makes it no death at all.
He accordingly fuppofes it to confift in the
falling off of man; when the divine Logos,
the great High Prieft, withholds his falutary
influence, and man is quite deferted. [1] Ἑως
γαρ ὁ ἱερωτατος ὗτος Λογος ζη και περιεϛιν εν
ψυχη—*For as long as the divine Logos lives
and prefides in the human foul,* there is no
guilt; no appearance of fin: but when he
withdraws himfelf, then commences fin and
corruption. But this is the fpiritual death
of the man, and not the death of the Logos,
who could neither fuffer, nor die. He is
reprefented by Philo himfelf, as *the Son of
God, before the Angels, before all worlds,* and
αἰδιος, *everlafting*—Σφραγις Θεꝟ— ἡς ὁ χαρακτηρ
ὁ αἰδιος Λογος. The Author in confequence
of it is forced to compromife the matter,
and fo to qualify his words, as fcarcely to
leave any fenfe. [2] Ἐαν δε αποθανη (ὁ Αρχιερευς
Λογος), ꝯκ αυτος διαφθαρεις—*When the Logos
fhall die, who is not fufceptible of death or corruption*—then, at this crifis *of death without*
dying,

[1] De Profugis, V. i. p. 563. l. 27.

[2] Ibid. l. ꝯr.

dying, the freedom of man is to commence.
But this way of reafoning is too vague and
inconfiftent to be admitted. It is plain, that
Philo had accefs to a noble repofitory; from
which he borrowed fome very excellent ma-
terials; but failed greatly in the application.

XL.

The neceffity of a Redeemer, and ranfom
for fin.

Though Philo could not admit of a crucified Meffiah, yet he allows, and adopts,
moft of the falutary articles relating to Chrift
in his ftate of manhood: by which we may
learn, how very reafonable they appeared to
him. But at the fame time he mifapplies
them, and refers them either to the Logos
in his heavenly ftate, or elfe to the fupreme
Deity, to whom they cannot be applied. We
have feen, that he fpeaks of fin, and *the
propitiation for fin*; alfo of the λυτρα και
σωςρα — *the price and ranfom for iniquity* —
and the means of falvation, by which fpiritual freedom is to be obtained here, and

ever-

everlafting life hereafter. But thefe bleffings he fuppofes to arife from acts and ordinances, which were not adequate; fuch as the fin-offerings, and other oblations, which were prefented in the Temple, but were not fufficient for that great purpofe. He fometimes feems to acknowledge, that thefe oblations were types, and that the High Prieft himfelf, who made interceffion, was merely a reprefentative of a greater Perfonage, from whom thefe bleffings were to be derived. At other times he thinks, that mere repentance without fatisfaction is fufficient: ¹Τ𝑣τ' εϛιν αφεϲις, τ𝑣τ' ελευθερια. ² Ἡ κακωϲις αυτη ιλαϲμος εϛι. *To repent affords remiffion of fins. Humility produces propitiation.* Still he acknowledges, that there muft be additionally fome oblations made, and fome victims offered to divine juftice. On thefe he founds our reconciliation with the offended Deity; alfo on the rectitude of the Priefts and Levites, by whom the offerings were madè.

He

' De Congreffu, &c. V. 1. p. 534. l. 43. See alfo p. 84.

IN L. . V 1 1. . 35.

He ſtyles theſe oblations ἱλασμὸς; and the altar [1] ἱλαστηριον, *or the ſeat of mercy,* and propitiation: and mentions the Levites as [2] Λυτρα των αλλων ἁπαντων — *a propitiation for all the people.* Both repentance and offerings were requiſite, and the miniſtering of the Prieſts neceſſary: but they were only figurative, and of themſelves could not effect atonement and reconciliation. Something of more conſequence was wanting.

Philo in thus proſecuting his opinion ſeems to approximate to the truth: but his ſtrong prejudices were a conſtant obſtacle; and would not ſuffer him to admit it in full force. Yet he ſometimes makes wonderful conceſſions, as may be ſeen in many extracts, which I have produced from him; and eſpecially in the following inſtance. He is ſpeaking of the neceſſity of a Mediator, to whom all in the ſervice of God ſhould apply.

Αναγκαιον

[1] De Profugis, V. i. p. 561. l. 13.

[2] De Sacrificiis, V. i. p. 186. l. 25.

L

¹Αναγκαιον γαρ ην τον ἱερωμενον τω τε κοσμυ
Πατρι Παρακλητω χρησθαι τελειοτατω την αρετην
υἱω, προς τε αμνησιαν ἁμαρτηματων, και χορηγιαν
αφθονωτατων αγαθων. *For it was neceffary for
a perfon, who was performing his duty to the
great Father of the world, to apply to his Son*
(the Logos) *as an advocate the moft perfect in
every virtue, both to have his fins forgotten,
and for the obtaining of every good gift.* One
would imagine, that he had feen the Epiftles
of St. John, and alluded to them. ² Τεκνια
μυ, ταυτα γραφω ὑμιν, ἱνα μη ἁμαρτητε. Και
εαν τις ἁμαρτη, Παρακλητον εχομεν προς τον Πατερα, Ιησυν Χριςον, δικαιον· και αυτος ἱλασμος εςι
περι των ἁμαρτιων ἡμων. *My little children,
thefe things I write unto you, that ye fin not.
But if any man fin, we have an advocate with
the Father, Jefus Chrift, the righteous* (τελειο-
τατον την αρετην): *and he is the propitiation for
our fins.* His words feem to be a comment
upon the Apoftle.

XLI. OF

---

¹ De Mofe, V. ii. p. 155. l. 25.

² 1 John ii. 1.

XLI.

OF PHILO'S GREAT MISTAKE.

He complains juftly of the degeneracy of mankind, and prevalence of wickednefs; and adds — [1] Τις δ' εκ αν των ευ φρονεντων τα των πολλων ανθρωπων ιδων εργα, ... μη σφοδρα κατηφηση, και προς τον μονον Σωτηρα Θεον εκ-βοηση; ινα τα μεν επικεφιση· Λυτρα δε και σωςρα καταθεις της ψυχης, εις ελευθεριαν αυτην εξεληται. *What man is there of true judgment, who, when he fees the deeds of moft men, is not ready to call aloud to the great Saviour God, that he would be pleafed to take off this load of fin, and by appointing a price and ranfom for the foul, reftore it to it's original liberty?*

This—λυτρον και σωςρον—*ranfom and price of redemption*, was paid by the Son of God, as had been foretold by Ifaiah, and other Prophets; and he on that account was efteemed

[1] De Confufione Ling. V. i. p. 418. l. 47.

efteemed the true Saviour of the world. He
offered himfelf for a propitiatory facrifice;
and by him the true freedom of the foul was
obtained. *Surely our infirmities he hath borne,
and our forrows he hath undergone. He was
wounded for our tranfgreffions; was fmitten
for our iniquities — and by his bruifes we are
healed.*[1] This redemption was effected by
the Meffiah Chrift, who was a ftumbling
block to Philo and his nation, and unfor-
tunately rejected by them. Our Saviour
himfelf declared openly, that he came into
the world — [2]δεναι την ψυχην αυτε λυτρον
αντι πολλων — *to give his life as a ranfom
for many.* And St. Paul fays — [3]Χριςος
Ιησες .. ὁ δες ἑαυτον αντιλυτρον ὑπερ παντων
— *Jefus Chrift, who gave himfelf a ranfom
for all.* This was not properly the Logos,
as Philo feems to think: for the Word
of God in heaven cannot fuffer, nor be
facrificed. But it was — [4]Ανθρωπος Χριςος
Ιησες ... μεσιτης Θεν και ανθρωπων — *the man
Jefus*

[1] Ifaiah liii. 5.   [2] Matt. xx. 28.

[3] , T :: 6   [4] !::: .. 5

Jefus Chrift, the one Mediator between God and men. Hence he is miftaken, when he fays — ¹ Λεγομεν δε τον Αρχιερεα κκ ανθρωπον — *The High Prieft is not a man.* For all that was loft by one man was to be repaired by another. The heathen had fome traditional knowledge of this, as appears by the oracle,

Και κεφαλας Κρονιδη, και τω Πατρι πεμπετε φωτα.

This by a miftake became the foundation of human facrifices; of which cuftom Philo himfelf takes notice. But he makes all true expiation to center within the precinĉts of the Jewifh Temple, and to be compleated in their rites and offerings; through the interceffion of the High Prieft, the reprefentative of the Logos. To Chrift the Redeemer, the Word of God in a ftate of humanity, he paid no regard: nor could he conceive, that there was ² *a fecond man, the laft Adam, who was the Lord from heaven.* He trufted to the law, and the ordinances eftablifhed by that law: not knowing that

the

---

¹ V. i. p. 562. l. 13.   ² 1 Corinth. xv. 45. 47.

the law was only — ¹ σκιαν των μελλοντων
αγαθων — *the shadow of good things to come* —
Ουδεποτε δυναται τυς προσερχομενυς τελειωσαι —
*It therefore could never make it's profelytes and
followers perfect.* Neither the Levite, nor
the High Prieft of the Levites, could make
atonement for the fins of the world. ²Αδυνατον
γαρ αιμα ταυρων και τραγων αφαιρειν αμαρτιας.
The blood of bulls and goats had no fuch
efficacy. They were types of a greater offering to be one day made: and God himfelf
had fhewn their infufficiency, and that there
was no real dependence upon them. *To
what purpose is the multitude of your facrifices
to me, faith the Lord. I am full of the burnt-
offerings of rams, and the fat of fed beafts.
I delight not in the blood of bullocks, or of
lambs, or of he-goats: bring no more vain
oblations.* ³ Philo did not confider, that the
daily facrifice was to be taken away, and the
ordinances of Mofes to ceafe; when the
Mefliah

---

¹ Heb. x. 1.   ² Ibid. v. 4.

³ Ifiah 11. and 12.

Meffiah Prince was to be cut off, and *not
for himſelf*, but *for the ſins of the whole
world.*[1] To ſuch evidence he was deaf;
and induſtriouſly avoids ever mentioning the
Meffiah, whoſe emblem the anointed High
Prieſt was: and he ſeldom applies to the
Prophets, by whom the Meffiah was foretold.

XLII.

PHILO'S NOTION OF THE RETURN OF THE DISPERSED JEWS.

He could not be perſuaded, that this
great Perſonage had appeared, and been-
rejected by the Jews: of whoſe blindneſs
he partook and was a tacit abettor of their
crime. Inſtead of apprehending any evil,
that would enſue, he anticipates much
happineſs; and ſeems to think, that the
reſtoration of his brethren, diſperſed among
the Gentiles, was not far off, and that they
ſhould

[1] Dan. ix. 26.

should experience the good will of the Deity — ' Ευμενειας τευξονται της εκ τε σωτηρος και ιλεω Θεε..... Καν γαρ εν εσχατιαις ωσι γης δελευοντες παρα τοις αιχμαλωτες αυτες απαγεσιν εχθροις, ωσπερ αφ' ἑνος συνθηματος ἡμερα μια παντες ελευθερωθησονται· της αθροας προς αρετην μεταβολης καταπληξιν εργασαμενης τοις δεσποταις. Μεθησονται γαρ αυτες, αιδεσθεντες κρειτ]ονων αρχειν — *They will experience the goodness of the Saviour and merciful God. For though they may be in a state of flavery, and have been carried captive by their enemies to the farthest parts of the earth, yet they will all, as it were upon a signal given, be set free in one day. For their general return to virtue will be matter of universal wonder to their masters.* Μεθησονται γαρ αυτες, αιδεσθεντες κρειτ]ονων αρχειν. *They will send them back free to their country, and be ashamed any longer to rule over persons so superiour to themselves.* He then proceeds to mention their return from Greece, and other places, and of their being conducted by a divine Personage in appearance far beyond any thing, that the eye

ı De Exerat. V. ii. p. 435. l. 26.

eye of mortal ever beheld: who would be perceptible to them, but invifible to the reft of the world. Then their land was to be replenifhed, and happinefs and honour to be their portion: and a fuperabundance of good things was to enfue —[1] καθαπερ αενναων πηγων τȣ Θεȣ χαριτων ρεȣσαι — *as flowing from the everlafting fountain· of God's grace and goodnefs.* In fhort he mentions his brethren as the only future objects of God's loving-kindnefs; and reprefents the reft of the world as under a curfe — [2]Τρεψει γαρ ὁ Θεος τας αρας επι τȣς .... εχθρȣς — *God will turn all his wrath againft their· enemies.* This illufion prevailed, and thefe fair profpects were entertained, at the very time, when the clouds were gathering, and a ftorm impending, which foon burft upon this devoted people, and terminated in their utter ruin. So far from any return of the captive tribes, the whole Jewifh nation faw their city taken, their temple ruined, and their land

[1] De Execrat V. ii. p. 436. l. 25.

[2] Ibid. l. 28.

land made defolate. And they were themfelves driven away, to join their apoftate
brethren in foreign lands, and to fmart
under a long and painful captivity. Whether Philo lived fufficiently long to fee all
his views rendered abortive, and to have
fhared in thefe calamities, is uncertain.
He certainly approached towards the time
of this crifis.

SOME REMARKABLE DOCTRINES OF PHILO,

WITH PARALLEL PASSAGES FROM THE

EVANGELISTS AND APOSTLES.

XLIII.

Of natural impurity to be cleanfed and
wafhed away by divine influence only.

—παραχωρευντας τῳ Θεῳ το φαιδρυνειν, και
μηδεποτε νομισαντας ἱκανες ειναι ἑαυτες ανευ θειας
επιφροσυνης των κηλιδων αναμεσον εκνιψαι και
απολεσαι βιον.[1]

It

---

[1] De Somniis, V. i. p. 662. l. 37.

It is our duty to truſt to God to cleanſe and beautify our frame, and not to think, that we are of ourſelves capable, without his heavenly grace, to purge and waſh away the ſpots, with which our nature abounds.

John xv. 5. Χωρις εμυ υ δυνασθε ποιειν υδεν.
Without me ye can do nothing.

John iii. 5. Εαν μη τις γεννηθη εξ ὑδατος και πνευματος, υ δυναται εισελθειν εις την βασιλειαν τυ Θευ.
Except a man be born of water and of the ſpirit, he cannot enter into the kingdom of God.

1 Theſſ. v. 23. Αυτος δε ὁ Θεος της ειρηνης ἁγιασαι ὑμας ὁλοτελεις.
And the very God of peace ſanctify you wholly.

Titus iii. 3—5. Ημεν γαρ ποτε και ἡμεις ... δυ-λευοντες επιθυμιαις και ἡδοναις ποικιλαις ... αλλα (Σωτηρ ἡμων Θεος) κατα τον αυτυ ελεον εσωσεν ἡμας δια λυτρυ παλιγγενεσιας και ανακαινωσεως πνευματος ἁγιυ.

For

For we ourfelves alfo were fome-
times .... ferving divers lufts
and pleafures .... but God our
Saviour .... according to his
mercy faved us by the wafhing
of regeneration, and renewing
of the Holy Ghoft.

1 Cor. vi. 11. Αλλα απελυσασθε, αλλα ἡγι-
ασθητε, αλλα εδικαιωθητε εν τῳ
ονοματι τυ Κυριυ Ιησυ, και εν τῳ
πνευματι τυ Θευ ἡμων.

But ye are wafhed, but ye are
fanctified, but ye are juftified
in the name of the Lord Jefus,
and by the fpirit of our God.

1 John i. 9. Εαν ἱμολογωμεν τας ἁμαρτιας
ἡμων, πιςος εςι, και δικαιος, ἱνα αφῃ
ἡμιν τας ἁμαρτιας, και καθαρισῃ
ἡμας απο πασης αδικιας.

If we confefs our fins, he is
faithful and juft to forgive us
our fins, and to cleanfe us
from all unrighteoufnefs.

I cannot

I cannot help subjoining another passage from Philo, in which he takes notice of spiritual purification, and the necessity of having our sins washed away.

Βυληθεις μεντοι (ὁ Θεος) και της Θειας αρετης απ' Ουρανυ την εικονα επι γην καταπεμψαι δι' ελεον τε γενυς ἡμων, ἱνα μη ατυχηση της αμεινονος μοιρας, συμβολικως την ἱεραν Σκηνην και τα εν αυτη κατασκευαζει, σοφιας απεικονισμα και μιμημα. Της γαρ ακαθαρσιας ἡμων εν μεσω φησι την Σκηνην ἱδρυσασθαι, το λογιον, ἱνα εχωμεν ᾧ καθαρθησομεθα, εκνιψαμενοι και απολεσαμενοι τα καταρρυπαινοντα ἡμων τον αθλιον, και δυσκλειας γεμοντα, βιον.[1]

§*

For, when it pleased God to send down from heaven the likeness of celestial virtue, out of pity to mankind, that they might not hereafter fail of a better lot, he thought proper to appoint emblematically a sacred tabernacle, and to furnish it with various articles: which tabernacle was a type and resemblance of divine wisdom.

[1] Quis Rer. Divin. Hæres. V. i. p. 488. l. 39.

wifdom. For he tells us, that he placed this tabernacle, the feat of his oracle, in the midft of our ¹impurities, that we might have wherewithal to cleanfe ourfelves, and wafh away all the filth and pollution of our wretched, and ignoble being.

Our infirmities are very truly described by Philo, and the neceffity of purification. But this was not to be effected by a worldly tabernacle; but by a great High Prieft, of whom he has elfewhere taken notice; and who has once for all entered into a heavenly tabernacle, of which this was only an emblem. The High Prieft was Chrift himfelf — των αγιων λειτεργος, και της σκηνης της αληθινης, ην επηξεν ὁ Κυριος, και εκ ανθρωπος ² — *a minifter of the fanctuary, and of the true tabernacle, which the Lord pitched, and not man.*

The

ʳ Leviticus xvi. 16. The Editor interprets this paffage otherwife.

ª Heb. viii. 2.

The former ordinances were ineffectual,
—μονον επι βρωμασι και πομασι, και διαφοροις
βαπτισμοις, και δικαιωμασι σαρκος, μεχρι καιρε
διορθωσεως επικειμενα. Χριςος δε παραγενομενος
Αρχιερευς των μελλοντων αγαθων, δια της μειζονος
και τελειοτερας Σκηνης, ε χειροποιητε, τετεςιν,
ε ταυτης της κτισεως ... εισηλθεν εφαπαξ εις τα
ἁγια, αιωνιον λυτρωσιν ἑυραμενος.[1]

— which flood only in meats and drinks, and
divers washings, and carnal ordinances, impofed
upon them to the time of reformation.

But Chrift being come, an High Prieft of
good things to come, by a greater and more
perfect tabernacle, not made with hands, that
is to fay, not of this building ......hath
entered once into the holy place, having obtained eternal redemption for us.

XLIV. Of

[1] Heb. ix. 1c, 11, 12.

XLIV.

Of our beſt works not being of themſelves
acceptable, nor of value, but through the
goodneſs of God — Μηδε την αρετην, ανευ θειας
επιφροσυνης, ἱκανην εξ ἑαυτης ωφελειν ειναι [1] —
*Even virtue without God's ſanction can never
profit us.*

Rom. viii. 8.   'Οι εν σαρχι οντες Θεω αρεσαι ʊ
δυνανται.

          *They, that are in the fleſh,
cannot pleaſe God.*

1 Peter ii. 5.   . . . . ευπροσδεκτες τω Θεω δια
Ιησʊ Χριςʊ.

          *. . . . acceptable to God through
Jeſus Chriſt.*

Heb. xii. 28.   Εχωμεν χαριν, δι' ἡς λατρευωμεν
ευαρεςως τω Θεω.

          *Let us have grace, whereby we
may ſerve God acceptably.*

Rom.

---

[1] De Deteriore—inſidiando, V. i. p. 203. l. 18.

Rom. iii. 24. ... δικαιυμενοι δωρεαν τη αυτυ χαριτι δια της απολυτρωσεως της εν Χριςω Ιησυ, ὁν προεθετο ὁ Θεος ἱλαςηριον.

Being justified freely by his grace, through the redemption, that is in Jesus Christ, whom God hath set forth to be a propitiation.

2 Tim. i. 9. ... Θευ τυ σωσαντος ἡμας και καλεσαντος ... υ κατα τα εργα ἡμων, αλλα κατ᾽ ιδιαν προθεσιν και χαριν.

God, who hath saved us, and called us, ... not according to our works, but according to his own purpose, and grace.

Rom. xv. 16. ... Προσφορα ... ευπροσδεκτος, ἡγιασμενη εν πνευματι ἁγιω.

An offering acceptable, being sanctified by the Holy Ghost.

XLV. Of

XLV.

Of Faith in God, the first requisite.

Μονος δ' αποδοχης αξιος, ο αναθεις την ελπιδα
Θεω, και ως αιτιω της γενεσεως αυτης, και ως
ασινη και αδιαφθορον ικανω μονω διαφυλαξαι.
*That man is only worthy of acceptation, who
places his hope in God, as the Author of his
being; and as the only one, who is able to keep
him free from sin and corruption.*[1]

. . . . ως δεον μηδενα νομιζεσθαι τοπαραπαν
ανθρωπον, ος αν μη επι Θεον ελπιζη.
*Nobody should be looked upon as at all human,
that does not place his trust in God.*[2]

Προς το Ον πιςιν . . . την βασιλιδα των αρετων.
Faith in God, the most noble of all virtues.[3]

Heb.

[1] De Præmiis, &c. V. ii. p. 410. l. 24.

[2] Ibid. l. 34.

[3] De Abrahamo, V. ii. p. 39. l. 18.

Heb. xi. 6.   Χωρις δε πιςεως αδυνατον ευαρεσ-
τησαι.
*Without faith it is impossible to
please him.*

Mark xi. 22.   Ὁ Ιησυς λεγει αυτοις, Εχετε πιςιν
Θευ.
*Jesus answering saith unto
them, Have faith in God.*

Rom. iii. 28.   Λογιζομεθα υν πιςει δικαιυσθαι
ανθρωπον χωρις εργων νομυ.
*Therefore we judge, that a man
is justified by faith without the
deeds of the law.*

Rom. v. 1.   Δικαιωθεντες υν εκ πιςεως, ειρηνην
εχομεν προς τον Θεον δια τυ
Κυριυ ἡμων Ιησυ Χριςυ.
*Therefore being justified by
faith, we have peace with God,
through our Lord Jesus Christ.*

XLVI. Of

XLVI.

Of the nature of Faith, and of it's very
falutary confequences according to Philo.

In the Old Teftament we find a belief of
God, and a truft in his providence, with a
fubmiffion to his divine will, continually
recommended. But the duty of Faith, and
the bleffings, with which it is attended, were
never fo defcribed, and enforced, as we find
them to have been afterwards by the Evangelifts and Apoftles. Thefe excellent perfons
have taught us, in what it confifts, and the
virtues, with which it fhould be accompanied; the peace alfo and comfort, with
which it is attended here; and the everlafting happinefs, which it will produce hereafter. This happinefs depends on our Faith
in Chrift, THE WORD OF GOD: on him it is
exprefly founded. But concerning this we
have no fure light afforded either from the
Law,

Law, or from the Prophets. From the sacred Writers afterwards we learn, that without faith, and faith in Christ — αδυνατον ευαρεςησαι (τω Θεω) — *it is impossible to please God.*[1] By faith we are justified:[2] By faith sanctified:[3] By faith made wise to salvation:[4] Through faith we are saved:[5] The propitiation for our sins obtained through faith.[6] By this faith in Christ the disciples had power to cast out devils — εξυσιαν εκβαλλειν τα δαιμονια.[7] — Κυριε, και τα δαιμονια ὑποτασσεται ἡμιν εν τω ονοματι σε. — *Lord, even the devils are subject to us in thy name.*[8] They were likewise enabled to improve themselves in all that was good; and to preserve themselves — ἁγιυς, και αμωμυς, και ανεγκλητυς — *holy, unblameable, and unreproveable,* if they remained — τη πιςει τεθεμελιωμενοι — *well established*

---

[1] Heb. xi. 6.

[2] Galat. ii. 16.

[3] Acts xxvi. 18.

[4] 2 Tim. iii. 15.

[5] Ephes. ii. 8.

[6] Rom. iii. 25.

[7] Mark iii. 15.

[8] Luke x. 17.

blifhed in faith.[1] Whatever they afked in faith, and in the name of Chrift, they were to obtain. Εαν εχητε πιςιν . . . . παντα, ὁσα αν αιτησητε εν τη προσευχη, πιςευοντες ληψεσθε. *If ye have faith . . . . all things, whatfoever ye fhall afk in prayer, believing, ye fhall receive.*[2] Εαν τι αιτησητε εν τῳ ονοματι μυ, εγω ποιησω. *If ye fhall afk any thing in my name, I will do it.*[3] St. Paul tells us—Εςι δε πιςις ελπιζομενων ὑποςασις· πραγματων ελεγχος υ βλεπομενων— *Now faith is the foundation of things hoped for, the evidence of things not feen.*[4]

When therefore I fee Philo alluding to any of thefe doctrines, which were in a great degree unknown to the Jewifh Church, and to which the Gentiles were quite ftrangers, I know no fource, from which he could poffibly obtain them, except from the firft Chriftians of his time. His defcription of Faith is very remarkable.

Μονον

[1] Coloff. i. 22, 23. [2] Matt. xxi. 22.

[3] John xv. 14. [4] Heb. xi. 1

Μονον εν αψευδες και βεβαιον αγαθον ή προς τον
Θεον πιςις. παρηγορημα βιε, πληρωμα χρηςων
ελπιδων. αφορια μεν κακων, αγαθων δε φορα. κακο-
δαιμονιας¹ απογνωσις, ευσεβειας γνωσις. ευδαιμονιας
κληρος, ψυχης εν άπασι βελτιωσις, επερηρεισμενης
τω παντων αιτιω, και δυναμενω μεν παντα, βελο-
μενω δε τα αριςα.

*The only sure and wellfounded blessing, to which
we can trust, is faith in God. It is the
comfort of life, and comprehends every salutary hope. It is the diminution of evil, and
productive of all good: the ruin of demoniacal
influence,*

---

¹ Some interpret κακοδαιμονια, *unhappiness*; and it is
sometimes by the Author used in that acceptation. But
as it is here contrasted with ευσεβειας γνωσις, I should think,
that in this place it relates to foul illusions, and particularly to the influence of demons.

Aristophanes makes a person say to another, Τις αν εκ
ηγοιτ' ειναι μανιαν; κακοδαιμονιαν τε ετι μαλλον; *Who would not
think, that this was madness; or rather a diabolical frenzy?*
Plutus, v. 501.

In another place a man homouroufly says — Μη ε
κικλοφας, αλλ'ηρπακας. *You did not steal it: You only ran
away with it.* The other answers — κακοδαιμονεις — *You
are frantick* — Anglice — *The devil's in you.*
Plut. v. 372.

M 4

influence, and the promoter of true godlinefs.
It affords a title to happinefs, and is the im-
provement of the human foul; when the foul
repofes itfelf, and confides, in the great Author
of it's being; who can do all things, but wills
only, and determines, what is beſt.[1]

XLVII.

Of Repentance in confequence of Faith.

Δευτεραν δ' εχει ταξιν, μετα την ελπιδα, ἡ επι
τοις ἁμαρτανομενοις μετανοια.[2]

The next duty in order after faith is repent-
ance of our fins.

Μετα δε την ελπιδος νικην αγων δευτερος εςιν, εν
ᾧ μετανοια αγωνιζεται.[3]

When we have gained hope, the next conflict,
in which we are engaged, is to eſtabliſh re-
pentance.

Luke

[1] De Abrahamo, V. ii. p. 38. l. 49, &c.

[2] Ibid. V. ii. p. 3. l. 46.

[3] De Præmiis et Pœnis, V. ii. p. 410. l. 36.

Luke xiii. 3.　Ουχι, λεγω ὑμιν· αλλ᾽ εαν μη
μετανοητε, παντες ὡσαυτως απο-
λεισθε.

*I tell you nay: but except ye
repent, ye shall all likewise
perish.*

Acts ii. 38.　Μετανοησατε, και βαπτισθητω
ἑκαςος ὑμων.

*Repent, and be baptized every
one of you.*

Luke xxiv. 47.　Εδει . . . κηρυχθηναι επι τω ονοματι αυτε μετανοιαν και αφεσιν
ἁμαρτιων εις παντα τα εθνη.

*Repentance and remission of sins
should be preached in his name
among all nations.*

Rom. ii. 4.　Το χρηςον τε Θεε εις μετανοιαν
σε αγει.

*The goodness of God leadeth thee
to repentance.*

XLVIII. Of

XLVIII.

Of Righteoufnefs and good works, the confequence of repentance.

Μετα δε τ⸲ς της μετανοιας αγωνας τριτα αθλα τιθεται Δικαιοσυνης.[1]

After repentance the third confliet is to maintain righteoufnefs.

. Μετα την ελπιδα δευτεραν εχ⸲ι ταξιν μετανοια και Βελτιωσις· οθεν εξης αναγραφ⸲α τον απο χειρονος βι⸲ προς τον αμεινονα μεταβαλοντα.[2]

After faith comes repentance and improvement; in confequence of which we read of perfons, who from a bad life are converted to a better.

Acts xxvi. 20. . . . Εις πασαν τε την χωραν της Ι⸲δαιας, και τοις εθνεσιν, απηγγελλον μετανοειν, και επιςρεφειν επι τον Θεον, αξια της μετανοιας εργα πρασσοντας.

I fhewed

[1] V. ii. p. 411. l. 36.   [2] Ibid. p. ʒ. l. 46.

I fhewed . . . . throughout all the coafts of Judea, and then to the Gentiles, that they fhould repent, and turn to God, and ao works meet for repentance.

James ii. 18.   Δειξον μοι την πιςιν σε εκ των εργων σε.

Shew me thy faith by thy works.

James ii. 17.   . . . . ἡ πιςις, εαν μη εργα εχη, νεκρα εςι καθ᾽ ἑαυτην.

Faith, if it hath not works, is of itfelf dead.

James ii. 24.   Ὁρατε τοινυν, ὁτι εξ εργων δικαι-εται ανθρωπος, και εκ εκ πιςεως μονον.

Ye fee then, how that by works a man is juftified, and not by faith alone.

XLIX. Of

XLIX.

Of the mercies of the Saviour God, and of men's relation and affinity to the divine Word, through the goodnefs of God, upon their repentance, and good deeds, and confeffion of their fins.

Εαν μεντοι . . . . καταιδεσθεντες ολη ψυχη μεταβαλωσι, κακισαντες μεν αυτες της πλανης, εξαγορευσαντες δε και ὁμολογησαντες ὁσα ἡμαρτον καθ᾽ αυτες, διανοια κεκαθαρμενη το πρωτον εις το τε συνειδοτος αψευδες και ανυπελον, επειτα και γλωττη, προς βελτιωσιν των ακεοντων, ευμενειας τευξονται της εκ τε Σωτηρος και ἱλεω Θεε, τω γενει των ανθρωπων εξαιρετον παρασχομενε και μεγιςην δωρεαν, την προς τον αυτε Λογον συγγε- νειαν, αφ᾽ ε καθαπερ αρχετυπον γεγονεν ὁ ανθρω- πειος νες.[1]

If then they have from their very fouls a juft contrition, and are changed, and have humbled themfelves for their paft errors, ac-
knowledging

---

[1] De Execrationibus, V. ii p. 435. l. 29.

*knowledging and confessing their sins, having a
conscience purified first in sincerity and truth
to the power, who knows those sins, and afterwards by confession to those, who may be thereby
edified; such persons shall find pardon from the
Saviour and merciful God, and receive a most
choice and great advantage, of being made like
the Logos of God: who was originally the great
arche-type, after which the soul of man was
formed.*

Rom. vi. 5. Ει γαρ συμφυτοι γεγοναμεν τω
ὁμοιωματι τȣ Ѳανατȣ αυτȣ,
αλλα και της αναςασεως εσομεθα.
*For if we have been planted
together in the likeness of his
death, we shall be also in the
likeness of his resurrection.*

John xvii. 22. Και εγω την δοξαν, ἡν δεδωκας
μοι, δεδωκα αυτοις· ἱνα ωσιν ἑν,
καθως ἡμεις ἑν εσμεν. Εγω εν
αυτοις, και συ εν εμοι.
*And the glory, which thou
gavest me, I have given them;
that they may be one, even as we
are one. I in them, and thou in me.*

1 John

1 John iii. 2.   Αγαπητοι, νυν τεκνα Θεε εσμεν,
και ηπω εφανερωθη, τι εσομεθα.
Οιδαμεν δε, ότι, εαν φανερωθη,
όμοιοι αυτω εσομεθα.

*Beloved, we be now the sons of
God; and it doth not yet appear, what we shall be : but
we know, that, when he shall
appear, we shall be like him.*

1 Cor. xv. 49.   Και καθως εφορεσαμεν την εικονα
τε χοϊκε, φορεσομεν και την εικονα
τε επερανιε.

*And as we have borne the
image of the earthy, we shall
also bear the image of the
heavenly.*

L. Man

L.

Man the Temple of God.

Philo speaks of persons truly virtuous and holy, as being the temples of God.

'Ουτος (ὁ νες), ᾧ φησιν ὁ προφητης τον Θεον εμπεριπατειν, ὁια βασιλειῳ.

God dwells, as saith the prophet, in the rational part of man, the soul, as in a palace.[1]

Και γαρ ες τῳ Οντι βασιλειον και οικος Θεε, ·σοφε διανοια.

For the palace and temple of the great self-existing Deity is the intellectual portion of a man of wisdom.[2]

'Ο Θεος .... νεων αξιοπρεπεστερον επι γης ες ευρε λογισμε.

The Deity could never find upon earth a more excellent temple, than the rational part of man.[3]

Δυο

---

[1] De Præmiis et Pœnis, V. ii. p. 428, l. 10.

[2] Ib. l. 12.

[3] De Nobilitate, V. ii. p. 437. l. 11.

Δυο γαρ .... ἱερα Θεʊˑ ἐν μεν ὁδε ὁ κοσμος
.... ἑτερον δε λογικη ψυχη.

*There are two temples of God: one of which
is this world; the other is the rational soul.*[4]

1 Cor. iii. 16. Ουκ οιδατε, ὁτι ναος Θεʊ εςε, και
το πνευμα τʊ Θεʊ οικει εν ὑμιν;
*Know ye not, that ye are the
temple of God; and that the
spirit of God dwelleth in you?*

2 Cor. vi. 16. Ὑμεις γαρ ναος Θεʊ εςε ζωντος.
*Ye are the temple of the living
God.*

Eph. ii. 22. Εν ᾧ (Χριςῳ) και ὑμεις συνοικο-
δομεισθε εις κατοικητηριον τʊ Θεʊ.
*In whom ye also are builded to-
gether for an habitation of God.*

1 Pet. ii. 5. Και αυτοι ὡς λιθοι ζωντες οικοδο-
μεισθε, οικος πνευματικος .....
ανενεγκαι πνευματικας θυσιας.
*Ye also, as lively stones, are
built up a spiritual house ....
to offer up spiritual sacrifices.*

LI. HIS

---

[4] De Somniis, V. i. p. 653. l. 22.

LI.

His account of the firſt created Man.

Philo mentions man as formed after the image of God — κατ' εικονα Θεϗ; and that he was alfo to be efteemed the image of the Logos — αρχετυπον τϗ αιτιϗ Λογϗ. [1]

He ſtyles the firſt man Adam, and fays, that he was by God placed in Paradife; and that he was in a ſtate of perfection and freedom — Ειργασατο γαρ αυτον (ὁ Θεος) αφετον και ελευθερον [2] — *For God created him to be at large without comptroll, in a ſtate of full liberty.* But he difobeyed and was expelled, and forfeited his happinefs. [3] Here fin commenced; and a curfe was hence entailed upon his pofterity. He fell from his original brightnefs; and loft that likenefs, which he before held, of the Deity, who formed him.

Τοιγαρϗν

[1] De Plantatione, V. i. p. 332. l. 38.

[2] Quod Deus fit immutab. V. i. p. 280. l. 7.

[3] De Legum Alleg. V. i. p. 61. l. 38. p. 63. l. 10.

Τοιγαρυν υκ απωνατο[1] απο της λαμπρας
ευγενειας, επαρατος γενομενος, και τοις μετ᾽ αυτον
αρχη κακοδαιμονιας.[2]——*Hence he enjoyed little
advantage from his noble origin, having
brought a curse upon himself, and being the
author of unhappiness to all, who came after
him.*

Here we have a juft account of the fall
of man, and original fin, and it's fatal
confequences to the world——Εφ᾽ οις εικοτως
Θνητον αντ᾽ αθανατυ βιον ἀνθυπηλλαξατο[3]——
*From this immortal ftate he was juftly doomed
to death, and made a perifhable being.* After
Philo has mentioned this inherent evil in
the conftitution of man, one would expect,
that he would point out fome remedy, fome
proper atonement, by which God's favour
might be regained, and man juftified in his
fight. But, as we have feen, his recourfe
is only to confeffion, and repentance, and
the blood of victims, which can never of
themfelves

---

[1] So the Editor very properly reads.

[2] De Nobilitate, V. ii. p. 440. l. 11. See note r.

[3] It. l. l.

themselves be an adequate compensation for guilt. When a man has risen in rebellion against his prince, has infringed the most salutary laws, and been guilty of theft, murder, and accumulated wickedness, he may say, that he is sorry for it, and wishes it had not been done; and he may present a bull or a goat for the persons he has robbed or slain. But this will not suffice before an earthly president; much less before the great judge of the world, the God of all justice and truth. Something more was therefore requisite by way of pardon and atonement. Philo could not, from his situation, but know the great article of the Christian creed—*Salvation through Christ*; and that he was *the propitiation for sin*. He should also have known, that all the offerings of atonement, appointed by the law, were unavailing; and only figurative of the great atonement to come. His own Prophets had told him so; and their words had been fulfilled. He has however acknowledged some truths of great consequence, which are well worth our observation.

LII. Of

LII.

Of the Holy Spirit.

We have feen, that Philo entertained a
very high opinion of the Logos, or Word of
God; and has fallen very little fhort of the
truth. Whether he held the third perfon,
the Spirit of God, in the fame efteem, and
had as juft an idea of it, may demand fome
confideration. In his account of the creation, where it is faid, that the Spirit of God
moved upon the waters, he makes it only
coeval with light, and defcribes it as nothing
more than the element of air.[1] But in
other places he affoids a very different defcription. For when he fpeaks of this divine
Spirit refting upon the Seventy Elders,[2] he
defcribes it as infinite, and indivifible; and
ftyles it — πανσοφον Πνευμα[3] — *the fpirit of all
wifdom.* He afterwards proceeds, and fays,

Νυν

[1] De Mofe, V. i. p. 6. l. 36. and p. 265. l. 31.

[2] Numb. xi. 17.

[3] ⸒ ⸒ ᴄ G⸒ ⸒ ⸒ · ⸒ · ⸒ · ⸒ · ⸒

Νυν δε το επ' αυτω Πνευμα εςι το σοφον, το
Θειον, το ατμητον, το αδιαιρετον, το αςειον, το
παντη δι' ιλων εκπεπληρωμενον· οπερ ωφελεν,
ε βλαπτεται, μεταδοθεν ετερω, εδ' αυ προτεθεν
ελαττεται την συνεσιν, και επιςημην, και σοφιαν.
Διο δη πνευμα θειον μενειν μεν δυνατον εν ψυχη,
καταμενειν δε αδυνατον, ὡς ειπομεν [1] — *Now
this Spirit of God is a being of wisdom and
of a divine nature, indivisible, inseparable,
beautiful, in every respect throughout compleat.
When it profits, it is not impaired: when
given to another, it receives no loss in percep-
tion, knowledge, or wisdom. Wherefore this
divine Spirit, though it may reside in the human
soul, yet cannot remain continually, as I have
mentioned.* He gives a reason for the Holy
Spirit not always abiding with men, on
account of their impurity — δια το ειναι αυτες
σαρκας, μη δυνασθαι το θειον Πνευμα καταμειναι [2]
— *The divine Spirit cannot dwell with them
always, because they are carnal.* But the
moft

[1] De Gigantibus, V. i. p. 266. l. 21.

[2] Ibid. l. 35.

N 3

moſt particular deſcription of the Holy
Spirit is to be found in his obſervations upon the words of Moſes.[1]   An account is
there given of three Angels appearing to
Abraham, which Philo mentions as the
ſacred Trias: and he deſcribes the great
reverence of the Patriarch at the ſight of
them—Και γαρ Αβρααμ, μετα σπυδης και ταχυς
και προθυμιας πασης ελθων, παρακελευεται τῃ
αρετῃ Σαραι .... ἡνικα ὁ Θεος δορυφορυμενος ὑπο
δυειν των ανωτατω Δυναμεων, αρχης τε αυ και
αγαθοτητος, εἰς ων ὁ μεσος, τριττας φαντασιας
ενειργαζετο τῃ ὁρατικῃ ψυχῃ (τε Αβρααμ)—*For
it was with great earneſtneſs, expedition, and
zeal, that Abraham went and gave directions
to his wife Sarai — when God, eſcorted on each
ſide by two Perſonages from on high, whoſe
attributes were Power and Goodneſs, (the Divinity in the middle being in union with the
other two) impreſſed a threefold appearance
upon the ſoul of Abraham, who beheld them.*[2]

He has in ſome degree impaired theſe
truths by his ſophiſtry, which I paſs over.

His

[1] Gen. c. xviii.

[2] De Sacrificiis, V : p 173. l. 12

His opinion is however plain, that the reprefentation of thefe divine Perfonages, who attended upon the Deity, were two Powers from heaven, whom he diftinguifhes for their rule and dominion, as well as for their goodnefs. He farther adds — εἰς ων ὁ μεσος: by which to me it appears manifeft, that he means the ¹ unity of the third with the two preceding. And though he feems to give·the fupremacy to God, yet he fpeaks of them all three, as απεριγραφοι; by which is meant — *unlimited, infinite,* confequently *not to be circumfcribed —* ὧν ἑκαςη μεμετρηται μεν ʼδαμως · απεριγραφος γαρ ὁ Θεος, απεριγραφοι

και

---

¹ Otherwife, to fay that there were three perfons, and that he in the middle was one of them, would appear idle, and unneceffary. His meaning may be known from a paffage before quoted, concerning the Logos· Ὁ δ᾽ ὑπεραυω τʼτων Λογος Θειος . . . . αυτος εικων ὑπαρχων Θεʼ, των νοητων ἁπαξαπαντων ὁ πρεσʼβυτατος, ὁ εγγυτατʼ, μηδενος οʼτος μεθοριʼ διαςημματος, τʼ μονʼ, ὁ ἐςιν αψευδως, αφιδρυμενος. De Profugis, V. i. p. 561. l. 16. *For the divine Logos, being the very Image of God, is above all other intellectual Beings whatever. And he is placed the neareft, without the leaft interval, to that great Monad, who can only be faid truly to exift, and be felf-exifting.*

και αι Δυναμεις αυτε. [1] — He adds, that the whole was a myſtery, which was not to be treated of lightly — Και των τελειων μυςις γενομενη τελετων, μηδενι προχειρως εκλαλη τα θεια μυςηρια · ταμιευομενη δ᾽ αυτα, και εχεμυθουσα, εν απορρητω φυλαττη — *For when a perſon has been, as it were[2] initiated, and partaken of theſe extraordinary myſleries, he ſhould not be too forward to diſcloſe ſuch ſacred articles; but like a good Steward preſerve them in ſilence; and conceal them among the things, which ought not to be divulged.* [3] To the latter part I cannot by any means ſubſcribe. Whatever divine Truth is afforded, we must admit it, and bear witneſs of it to the world. Although it contains ſomething above human conception, ſtill it muſt be admitted, if delivered from undoubted authority: otherwiſe we act contrary to reaſon, and to general practice. For we allow thouſands of things,

for

[1] De Sacrificiis, V. i. p. 173. l. 18.

[2] He alludes to the myſteries of Greece, and to perſons initiated in them; and makes uſe of their terms.

[3] Ibid. l 3.

for which we cannot account; and act, as if their properties were well known. We may therefore fafely proclaim our faith, and maintain the doctrine afforded; though it may in fome refpects be above our apprehenfion.

CONCLUSION.

If then we admit thefe doctrines of Philo, and excufe his prejudices and mifapplications, we fhall find fome wonderful truths afforded. And thefe could not be borrowed from his brethren, the Jews; for whatever knowledge they had of thefe myfteries, it was by no means adequate to the intelligence, which he has given. This muft have been obtained from the fource, to which I have referred it — from the fountain of all truth, the Gofpel; and from thofe excellent perfons, the immediate difciples of Chrift, in whofe time he lived; particularly from thofe, by whom fome of the firft churches were founded; and moft particularly from
the

the founder of the church of Alexandria,
where he refided. I muſt therefore repeat,
what cannot be too often urged, that in
him we read the ſentiments of the moſt
early Chriſtians, and of the Apoſtles themſelves.

Whence elſe could he have obtained ſo
many terms, which bear ſuch an analogy
with the expreſſions and doctrines in the
Apoſtolical Writings? Such are Ῑιος Θεﬄ,
Λογος πρωτογονος, πρεσϐυτατος, αιδιος, Λογος
Αρχιερευς, μεσος, μεθοριος, ἱκετης τﬦ Θνητﬦ, δημι-
ﬦργος, Ποιμην της ἱερας αγελης, Ῑπαρχος Θεﬦ,
σφραγις, εικων Θεﬦ, φως, πνευμα Θεﬦ, πνευμα
πανσοφον. We read farther concerning Redemption, and — λυτρα και σωςρα — *the price*
and ranſom for the ſoul, αντι Θανατﬦ ζωην αιδιον,
and νﬦς ανθρωπﬦ ναος Θεﬦ. To theſe other
inſtances might be added equally ſignificant:
few of which are to be found in the Greek
Verſion, or in any Jewiſh doctrines, at leaſt
in the acceptation here given. They were
obtained either from the converſation, or
from the writings, of the firſt Chriſtians; or
rather from both.

A LIST OF SOME OF THE PARTICULAR
TERMS AND DOCTRINES FOUND IN PHILO.

1. The Logos is the Son of God.
2. The fecond divinity.
3. The firft-begotten of God.
4. Εικων, or Image of God.
5. Superiour to angels.
6. Superiour to all things.
7. By whom the world was created.
8. Ὑπαρχος Θεȣ.
9. Φως Κοσμȣ, the Light of the world.
10. Who only can fee God.
11. Who refides in God.
12. The moft ancient of God's works.
13. Efteemed the fame as God.
14. Αϊδιος, Eternal.
15. Beholds all things: οξυδερκεςατος.
16. He fupports the world.
17. Neareft to God without any feparation.
18. Free from all taint of fin.
19. Who prefides over the imperfect and weak.
20. The Logos, the Fountain of Wifdom.

21. A Meſſenger ſent from God.

22. Ἱκετης, or Advocate for man.

23. He ordered and diſpoſed all things.

24. The Shepherd of God's flock.

25. Of the power and royalty of the Logos.

26. The Phyſician, who heals all evil.

27. The (σφραγις, or) ſeal of God.

28. The ſure refuge of thoſe, who ſeek him.

29. Of heavenly food diſtributed by the Logos equally to all, who ſeek it.

30. Of men's forſaking their ſins, and obtaining ſpiritual freedom.

31. Of men's being freed by the Logos from all corruption.

32. The Logos mentioned by Philo not only as Ὑιος Θεȣ, but alſo — αγαπητον τεκνον — his beloved Son.

33. By what means a man may attain to ſpiritual happineſs.

34. Of good men admitted to the aſſembly of perſons made perfect, and free from corruption.

35. The juſt man advanced by the Logos to the preſence of his Creator.

36. The Logos the true High Prieſt.

37. Λογος

Some other remarkable doctrines in Philo.

49. Of men being made like to the divine Word by repentance and good deeds.
50. Men truly virtuous are the Temples of God.
51. Philo's account of the firſt man, and his diſobedience.
52. Of the Holy Spirit, and ſacred Trias.

OF THE MANNA, OR FOOD FROM HEAVEN.

The account given by Philo of the manna, mentioned by Moſes, [r] is extraordinary. Our Saviour, the Word of God, has taken notice of it, as a type of himſelf, and endeavoured to explain to the Jews, what was the latent meaning. *I am that bread of life. Your fathers did eat manna in the wilderneſs, and are dead. This is the bread, which cometh down from heaven; that a man*

may

*may eat thereof, and not die. I am the living
bread, which came down from heaven. If a
man eat of this bread, he shall live for ever:
and the bread, that I will give, is my flesh;
which I will give for the life of the world.*[1]

Philo speaks of it in the same mysterious,
but significant, manner—Ὁυτος εςιν ὁ αρτος, ἡ
τροφη, ἡν εδωκεν ὁ Θεος τη ψυχη προσενεγκασθαι,
το ἑαυτʒ ῥημα, και τον ἑαυτʒ Λογον—*This is the
bread, that nourishment, which God appointed
to be applied to the soul of man, even his
doctrine, and his word.*[2]

Ὁ μεν γαρ (ανθρωπος) τας οψεις ανατεινει προς
αιθερα, αφορων το Μαννα, τον Θειον Λογον, την
ʒρανιων φιλοθεαμονος ψυχης αφθαρτον τροφην.
*Man lifts his eyes to heaven, and beholds the
manna, which is a type of the Logos, or Word
of God; and which affords heavenly, and immortal, nutriment to the intelligent soul.*[3]

Ετι

---

[1] John vi. 48, &c.

[2] De Leg. Alleg. V. i. p. 121. l. 26.

[3] Quis Rer. Di · ҉ Ha҉ҽs, V. ı. ҉ ҉ 484. l 3.

Ετι τοινυν την ερανιον τροφην ψυχης, ην καλει Μαννα, διανεμει πασι τοις χρησομενοις Λογος Θειος εξ ισε. *Besides, this heavenly food of the soul, called manna, is distributed equally to all, who will make a good use of it, by the Logos, or Holy Word of God.*[1]

Ὁρας της ψυχης τροφην δια εςι; Λογος Θεε συνεχης. *Do you then see, what is meant by this nutriment of the soul, manna? Even the never-failing Word of God*[2] — Τετο το ῥημα, ὃ συνεταξε Κυριος; — *It is the doctrine, or word ordained by the Lord.*[3]

Την τροφην ταυτην ἑτερωθι ..... καλει Μαννα, τον πρεσβυτατον των οντων Λογον Θεον. *This heavenly food he elsewhere calls Manna; the same figuratively, as the first of all beings, the divine Logos, or Word.*[4]

Observations

---

[1] Quis Rer. Div. Hæres, V. i. p. 499. l. 44.

[2] De Leg. Alleg. V. i. p. 120. l. 34.

[3] Ibid. l. 33. and De Profugis, V. i. p. 566. l. 22.

[4] De l. i . \ . 211 . 45

OBSERVATIONS UPON THE OPINION OF
PHILO.

We find, that Philo explains the purport
of this heavenly Manna, by faying it was
Bread — Ὁυτος εϛιν ὁ αρτος τροφη—And this
bread, he fays, is that divine food, which
God hath fent for the nourifhment of the
human foul, even — το ἑαυτȣ ῥημα, και τον
ἑαυτȣ Λογον — *his divine doctrine, and his*
Λογος,—*or Word.* It is reprefented, as—ψυχης
την αφθαρτον τροφην — *the incorruptible food of
the foul*; which — Λογος Θεος διανεμει πασι εξ
ισȣ — *the heavenly Logos diftributes impartially
to all.* He in another place tells us in like
manner, that it was not only a doctrine,
but alfo a perfon, that was alluded to under
this fymbol of bread, and heavenly food —
Μαννα . . . . τον ωρεσϐυτατον των οντων Λογον
Θειον — By this Manna was fignified *the moft
ancient of beings, the facred Logos :* whom he
elfewhere has ftyled — ὁ δευτερος Θεος — *the
fecond Divinity.*

O

Such

Such is the folution of the myftery concerning the heavenly bread, the food of the
foul, which was afforded to the Ifraelites
in the wildernefs. From this interpretation,
I think, it is manifeft, that he was beholden
to the account given of our Saviour's words
by fome of the Difciples, and Apoftles; the
fame, which occurs in ¹ St. John, chap. vi.
The correfpondence of fentiment feems to
evince it; however he may in fome refpects
have varied from the true fcope of the
doctrine. The following extracts will perhaps illuftrate, what I fay; and fhew, that
Philo

---

¹ It may poffibly be doubted, whether Philo had this
account from the Gofpel of St. John, as he might not
perhaps live long enough to have feen it. But though
this doctrine is only tranfmitted to us by St. John, yet
we muft not imagine, that it was known to him only.
They are the words of Chrift, which he fpake openly;
and which muft have been known to all, who heard
him. And whoever applied to his Difciples and Apoftles,
might eafily be acquainted with them. Philo perhaps
had them from St. Mark. St. John's Gofpel was written before the deftruction of Jerufalem; at which time
Philo was probably about fixty-eight years old. and he
fpeaks of himfelf, as living to be old and grey. It is
therefore not impoffible, but that he might have feen
c··· ··· C · ··· ·· · ···

Philo came very near the mark, when he called Manna — *της ψυχης υρανιον, αφθαρτον τροφην* — *the heavenly, incorruptible, and everlasting food of the soul, the bread from above.*

THE WORDS, AS WE FIND THEM IN THE GOSPEL OF ST. JOHN vi. 48.

Εγω ειμι ὁ αρτος της ζωης. Ὁι πατερες ὑμων εφαγον το μαννα εν τη ερημω, και απεθανον. Ὁυτος εςιν ὁ αρτος ὁ εκ τυ υρανυ καταβαινων, ἱνα τις εξ αυτυ Φαγη, και μη αποθανη. Εγω ειμι ὁ αρτος, ὁ ζων, ὁ εκ τυ υρανυ καταβας. John vi. 48, &c.

Ὁυτος εςιν ὁ αρτος, ὁ εκ τυ υρανυ καταβας· υ καθως εφαγον ὁι πατερες ὑμων το μαννα, και απεθανον. Ὁ τρωγων τυτον τον αρτον ζησεται εις τον αιωνα. v. 58.

Εργαζεσθε μη την βρωσιν την απολλυμενην, αλλα την βρωσιν την μενυσαν εις ζωην αιωνιον, ἡν ὁ υιος τυ ανθρωπυ ὑμιν δωσει. v. 27.

" I am

" I am the bread of life.

" Your fathers did eat manna in the wildernefs, and are dead.

" This is the bread, which cometh down from heaven; that a man may eat thereof, and not die.

" I am the living bread, which came down from heaven.

" This is the bread, which came down from heaven: not as your fathers did eat manna, and are dead. He that eateth of this bread fhall live for ever.

" Labour not for the meat, which perifh-eth; but for that meat, which endureth to everlafting life; which the fon of man fhall give unto you."

THE DIFFERENCE BETWEEN THE DOC-TRINES OF THE APOSTLES AND OF PHILO BRIEFLY STATED.

It is manifeſt, that Philo entertained the ſame high opinion of the ſecond Perſon, the δευτερος Θεος, as the Apoſtles, and Diſciples of Chriſt, and allows him the ſame attributes. His only failing is, in not allowing, that the Logos appeared in the fleſh, and con-ſequently had two natures, a divine and human, and two characters, which ſhould not be confounded. But Philo takes all the attributes of each character, and adapts them to one only. Hence he makes the Logos, not only the Image of God, and the Creator of the world; but alſo the Mediator and Redeemer of mankind, by whom the ranſom for ſin, and price of redemption, were paid: the ſame, who afforded heavenly food to the ſoul, and who was the Shepherd of God's choſen flock. Laſtly, he ſuppoſes him to have been the great High Prieſt, by whom interceſſion was made, and ſin

expiated;

expiated; and of whom Aaron with his
cenfer was a type. He therefore, as we
have feen, tells us — Λεγομεν εν Αρχιερεα εκ
ανθρωπον, αλλα Λογον θειον ειναι — and adds —
παντων αδικηματων αμετοχον — *I maintain, that
this High Prieft is not a man, but the divine
Word of God, the Logos, and that he is free
from all fin.* But he would more truly have
expreffed this doctrine by faying, Λεγομεν εν
τον Αρχιερεα ε κυριως τον Λογον Θειον ειναι, αλλα
Χρισον Ιησεν, τον υιον τε ανθρωπε, και τον Θεαν-
θρωπον, παντων αδικηματων αμετοχον. *I fay
then, that this High Prieft* (of whom Aaron
is reprefented as a type) *was not properly the
divine Logos, but Chrift Jefus, the Son of man,
both God and man, who did no fin;* but finlefs,
as he was, died for the fins of the world.
The whole character of our Saviour is
admitted by Philo, but tranfpofed, and
mifapplied.

THE GREAT CONSEQUENCE OF THE
EVIDENCE AFFORDED BY PHILO.

I have fhewn, that Philo was probably
born about the time of our Saviour's
coming into the world. It is certain, that
about eight years after the death of Chrift
he was fent from Alexandria ambaffador to
Rome; and furvived to the time of Nero.
I repeat this once for all to prove, that
he had opportunities of feeing, and con-
verfing with fome of the firft difciples of
the Apoftles, and even with the Apoftles
themfelves. We may go fo far as to conceive from his time of life and fituation,
(for he was born at Jerufalem) that he
might have had a fight of their great
Mafter. I fhould judge from many articles
in his writings, that he was not unacquainted with the three firft Gofpels: and
he either borrowed from them, or was
obliged for much knowledge to the Chriftians of his time. It is not improbable, but

o 4   that

that he had accefs to both. Hence his evidence in refpect to many great and important articles is of much confequence : for he fpeaks the language of the Apoftles, and of the firft teachers in the Church. The teftimony of the firft Greek Fathers has always been efteemed of great weight. But the evidence of Philo is attended with more efficacy, as well as certainty. For he was more early, than they, by many years; and lived, and wrote many of his Treatifes, before any errors had crept into the infant Church. And as he was no friend to Chriftianity, he could have no prejudices in favour of it: and we have feen, that thofe articles, which he has copied, and which have been produced, are agreeable to the doctrines of the Apoftles, excepting only fome mifapplications, of which mention has been made. Hence we cannot have a more fatisfactory proof of the purport of thofe doctrines, with the truth and fublimity of which he was captivated, and which he adopted for his own. We receive them through his hands, as we do the light of the

fun

fun reflected from a mirror — though not fo copious, nor fo powerful, as from the original; yet very genuine, and fufficient to fhew the fountain of light, from which they are derived.

CONCLUSION.

Let me then conclude in the words of the Apoftle St. Paul, when he gave fome very fignificant advice to the people and Church at Coloffe.[1]

Περιπατησαι ὑμας αξιως τɤ Κυριɤ εις πασαν αρεσκειαν, εν παντι εργω αγαθω καρποφορɤντες και αυξανομενοι ...,.. Ευχαριςɤντες τω Πατρι τω ἱκανωσαντι ἡμας εις την μεριδα τɤ κληρɤ των ἁγιων εν τω φωτι. Ὁς ερρυσατο ἡμας εκ της εξɤσιας τɤ σκοτɤς, και μετεςησεν εις την βασιλειαν τɤ ὑιɤ της αγαπης αυτɤ. Εν ᾡ εχομεν την απολυτρωσιν δια τɤ ἁιματος αυτɤ, την αφεσιν των ἁμαρτιων. Ὁς εςιν εικων τɤ Θεɤ τɤ αορατɤ, πρωτοτοκος

[1] Coloff. i. 10—&c.

¹ πρωτοτοκος πασης κτισεως. Ὁτι εν αυτω εκτισθη τα παντα, τα εν τοις ουρανοις, και τα επι της γης, τα ὁρατα, και τα αορατα, ειτε θρονοι, ειτε κυριοτητες, ειτε αρχαι, ειτε εξυσιαι. Τα παντα δι᾽ αυτε, και εις αυτον εκτισται. Και αυτος εςι προ παντων, και τα παντα εν αυτω συνεςηκε. Και αυτος εςιν ἡ κεφαλη τε σωματος της Εκκλησιας, ὁς εςιν αρχη, πρωτοτοκος εκ των νεκρων, ινα γενηται εν πασιν αυτος πρωτευων. Ὁτι εν αυτω ευδοκησε παν το ²πληρωμα κατοικησαι.

" 11. That

¹ I am perfuaded, from fome expreffions, of which the Apoftle makes ufe, that in this very particular defcription of the Second Perfon, he had an eye to the Jewifh Platonifts, and their opinions, which he here obviates. And I am equally perfuaded from the opinions of Philo, and the terms, in which they are couched, that he had feen St. Paul's Epiftles, efpecially that to the Coloffians, from which this abftract is made. A great part he adopted : and it would have been well, if he had copied the whole.

² A particular term of the Platonick Jews, by which they underftood and comprehended the whole hierarchy of heaven, and fometimes the whole fenfible and intellectual world

" 11. That we may walk worthy of the Lord unto all pleafing, being fruitful in every good work, and increafing in the knowledge of God.

" 12. Giving thanks unto the Father, which hath made us meet to be partakers of the inheritance of the Saints in light.

" 13. Who hath delivered us from the power of darknefs; and hath tranflated us into the kingdom of his dear Son.

" 14. In whom we have redemption through his blood, even the forgivenefs of fins.

" 15. Who is the image of the invifible God; the firft-born of every creature.

" 16. For by him were all things created, that are in heaven, and that are in earth, vifible and invifible: whether they be be thrones, or dominions, or principalities, or powers: all things were created by him, and for him.

" 17. And he is before all things; and by him all things confift.

" 18. And he is the head of the body, the Church; who is the beginning, the firft-born from the dead; that in all things he might have the pre-eminence.

" 19. For it pleafed the Father, that in him fhould all fulnefs dwell."

THE SENTIMENTS OF DR. ALLIX CONSIDERED.

Since I wrote this Treatife I have found, that, what has been faid by the learned Editor of Philo, concerning the birth, and age, of his Author, is entirely taken from that work of Dr. Allix, called "The Judgement of the ancient Jewifh Church againft the Unitarians." I am obliged to differ from this very refpectable Writer, as I have before from the Editor above-mentioned, who borrowed fo largely from him. His endeavour is to make Philo very much advanced in years in the reign of Caligula: which is the very time, as Photius' tells us, when he was in his prime. But to this point I have faid fo much, that there will be no occafion to make any addition. He allows, that Philo could not have borrowed his opinions from Plato, nor have obtained them from reafon: for they were beyond the wifdom of unaffifted Man. He

therefore

' C. cv. p. 278. l. 29. Εν τοις χρονοις (Φιλων) ηγμασι τε Γαιυ τε Κ?ι

s

therefore concludes, that they were derived
to him from the Jews; and tries to prove,
that they were fully poſſeſſed of this treaſure
of knowledge. He cannot believe, that
Philo had acceſs to any of the Apoſtles or
firſt Chriſtians on account of his great age:
for he ſuppoſes him to have been ſeventy
years old at the time of his [1] embaſſy. But
I have

[1] The Author's mode of argument.

" Joſephus in his Antiquities Lib. xviii. c. 10. aſſures
us, that Philo was the chief, and moſt conſiderable of
the Jews employed by thoſe of Alexandria in the Embaſſy to Caligula. This man, faith he, eminent among
thoſe of his nation, appeared before Caligula his death,
which was A.U.C. 793. that is to ſay, in the fourtieth
year of our Lord. Now Philo, in the hiſtory of his
legation to Caligula, ſays of himſelf, that he was at that
time all grey with age, that is 70 years old, according
to the Jewiſh notion of a man with grey hair, Pirke
Avoth. c. 5. Suppoſe then, that he was 70 years old,
when he appeared before Caligula, it follows, that he
was born in the year of Rome 723. Suppoſe alſo, that
he began to write at 30 years old, it will fall in with the
year of Rome 753: that is to ſay, 30 years before Chriſt
preached in Judea. For Jeſus Chriſt began not to
preach till the year of Rome 783." Dr. Allix. p. 80.

The whole of this depends upon one article taken for
granted, that Philo was 70 years old, when he went
upon this Embaſſy: for which there is not the leaſt
found

I have fhewn before, that almoft every page in the Treatife, upon which he founds his argument, evinces the contrary.

Another reafon urged by him to prove, that Philo was not beholden to Chriftians, is, becaufe he never mentions the name of Chrift. But why is this to be wondered at, if, after all that he borrowed, he continued ftill a Jew ? It fhould be confidered, that though he was of that race, he never once introduces the name of Jehovah, nor of the Meffiah, who about that time was much expected by the Jews. Nor does he take notice of feveral books, or writers, of the Old Teftament. When he went firft to Rome, it was to obviate all the calumnies, with which Apion of Egypt had loaded the Jewifh Nation. Yet in the hiftory of that tranfaction he never once mentions his name. We cannot therefore truft to inferences made from the filence of Philo. Juftus Tiberienfis was of Galilee, and in the time of our Saviour; and yet made no mention of Chrift or Chriftianity.

In

In confequence of this original miftake about the age of Philo, Dr. Allix proceeds throughout to fhew, that all thefe weighty truths, found in this Author, were obtained from his brethren the Jews, and are to be feen in their Mifna, Targums, and other books. In confequence of this he appeals continually to the compilers of thofe Writings to prove, that they held the fame opinions. But though he quotes largely from his extenfive learning; yet there are many great truths in Philo, neither mentioned by that Author, nor to be found among thofe Writers. Befides, the appeal is not well directed, and of little moment. For almoft every [1] Paraphrafe together with

the

---

[1] The moft early of thefe Writings is the Chaldee Paraphrafe of Onkelos, and the next is the Targum of Jonathan; which are fuppofed to have been compofed a few years before Chrift. But this refts merely upon Jewifh Traditions; which are not all uniform, and therefore very doubtful. The other Talmudim were much later. Anno a Templi Secundi incendio cxx — Mifna, Anno ccc — Talmud Hierofolymitanum. — Anno denique ccccxxxvi — Talmud Babylonicum. Galatini. l. 1. c. v. p. 13. See alfo Walton's Polyglott. Prolegomena p. 8 ` ` ;.

the Gemara, Mifna, Talmuds, and Targums, by whomfoever written, and under
whatever denomination, was later than
Philo. He was in great eftimation, and
they might copy from him; but he could
not well borrow from them. With fome
truths of confequence, and to the prefent
purpofe, the Jews were certainly acquainted.
They are to be found in their Sacred Writings. But there are others of equal moment, which could only be known by a later
Revelation. Thefe to a great amount are to
be found in Philo. As to the objection, that
he could not have had any intercourfe with
St. Mark, or with any of the Difciples of
Chrift, on account of his early time of
life, it has been fhewn from his own
evidence to have been an ill-grounded
notion.

P

A P P E N D I X

TO

P H I L O.

P A R T   III.

SOME OBSERVATIONS UPON PART OF A TREATISE WRITTEN BY THE Rev. CHARLES HAWTREY, M.A.[1]

I HAVE, and I think very juftly, recommended this Treatife.[2]   But there is one part, in which I cannot agree with the Author.   He there tries to prove, that Chrift in his ftate of manhood was the original Son of God; and that the Logos, or Word, antecedently was not his Son.   He accordingly fays, " Therefore it appears to

be

---

[1] This Treatife is entitled Θιανθρωπος της καινης διαθηκης, and was publifhed in 1794.

[2] In p. 57 of this work.

be the exprefs doctrine of the Evangelifts,
however it may have been overlooked, that
the filiation confifted, and confifted only,
in the Word's becoming flefh."[1] Again —
" The Logos, alfo, in uniting himfelf with
man's nature became the Son of God;[2]"
and was not the Son of God, as it is
intimated, prior to that union. For the
Author had faid before, (p. 40.) " That in
the birth of the Logos, in the union with
the σαρξ ανθρωπινη, confifted the filiation."

According to this doctrine, the Divine
Λογος, or Word of God, muft not be
efteemed the Son of God, till his appearance upon earth.

But how can we reconcile this with the
various paffages in the facred Writers,
wherein the contrary feems to be maintained? It is faid — that *God fent his only-
begotten Son into the world, that we might
live*

P. 41.   [2] Ibid.

live by him.[1] If he was the only-begotten Son of God, when he was fent, he muſt have been in that charaĉter, before he arrived; and his filiation was antecedent to his appearance upon earth.

It is faid again — *And we have feen, and do teſtify, that the Father fent the Son to be the Saviour of the World.*[2] I muſt therefore repeat the fame argument — If the Son of God was appointed, and fent, for a particular purpoſe, he muſt have exiſted in that charaĉter, before that purpoſe took place. Whoever is fent, muſt be antecedent to the fending; as appears from the words of our Saviour himſelf — *I proceeded forth, and came from God: neither came I of myſelf: but he fent me.*[3] And who was the perſon fent? We have feen before, that it was the *Son* of God by his proceeding

from

[1] 1 John iv. 9.

[2] Ibid. iv. 14.

[3] John viii. 42.

from *the Father*. The paſſages in Scripture
to this purpoſe are many. *God ſent his Son
in the likeneſs of ſinful fleſh;*[1] that is, in a
new character. It is plainly intimated, that
there was a time, when the Son was not in
the fleſh; but a divine Perſon without any
thing human. There is a remarkable inſtance in St. John,[2] where he mentions,
that they beheld *the glory of Chriſt*; and he
illuſtrates this by repeating the word *glory*,
and ſaying, *as of the only-begotten Son of the
Father*. The glory of Chriſt, we find, was
like that of the only Son of God. Chriſt
therefore in the fleſh was far poſteriour to
the Perſonage, to whom he is likened. His
appearance was ſuch, as one would expect
from the Logos, with whom he was united;
whoſe brightneſs he participated, as far as
fleſh and blood could partake. When it is
ſaid —[3]*All things, that the Father hath, are
mine* —[4]*And now, O Father, glorify thou me,*
with

[1] Rom. viii. 3.   [2] John i. 14.

[3] John xvi. 15.   [4] Ibid. xvii. 5.

with thine own felf with the glory, which I had with thee before the world was—can we fuppofe, that this paternity is to be dated from Chrift at Bethlehem, or Nazareth; or that it is to be limited to the age of Auguftus? As it was given by the Father before the creation, and the gift was to the Son, the filiation muft have commenced at that early feafon, when the Logos proceeded from the Father; *and being in the form of God, thought it not robbery to be equal with God; but made himfelf of no reputation, and took upon him the form of a fervant, and was made in the likenefs of men.*[1]

[1] Philip. ii. 6, 7.

OF OUR SAVIOUR BEGOTTEN BEFORE ALL WORLDS.

The Author fays in page 43, " I do not fee, how the γεννηθεντα προ παντων των αιωνων (*begotten before all worlds*) is to be fupported by any thing in the New Teftament." This feems extraordinary; becaufe it is faid, that Chrift, in his divine character, was—πρωτο-τοκος πασης κτισεως[1]—*the firft-born of every creature*; and antecedent to all worlds: for by him they were made.[2] He is alfo ftyled μονο-γενης, or *only-begotten· Son*. But Adam is called by St. Luke, iii. 38. the Son of God. There-fore this title of Son cannot be attributed to Chrift folely in his ftate of humanity: for there were others, as men, fo called before him. It relates to the only-begotten before all worlds. If therefore Chrift in the flefh is ever alluded to, as the firft-begotten, or only-begotten, of God, it arifes merely from his intimate union with the Logos, to whom this Title primarily belonged.

The

The learned Author is fenfible, that the paffage in Coloffians i. 15. makes againft his opinion: and he accordingly fays in the Appendix, p. 184, that " the words μονογενης and πρωτοτοκος are never any where in Scripture applied to the Λογος, but folely to the Υιος." But if the Logos and the Son are the fame, the objection amounts to nothing. But how can—πρωτο-τοκος πασης κτισεως—*the firfl-born of every creature*—be a character afcribed folely to Chrift in the flefh; who was thus mani-fefted fo long after that creation, in which he had been the great agent?

The Author ftill ftrives to rid himfelf of the difficulty, by fuppofing, that πρωτοτοκος, or *firfl-born*, fignifies here *the pre-eminence*, but not the *priority of his birth*, p. 185. But the word πρωτοτοκος can be made to fignify nothing more, nor lefs, than *firfl-begotten*, or firft-produced. And when it is faid of a perfon, that he was not only firft-begotten, but begotten before all created things, it muft relate to priority of exiftence, as well as to pre-eminence. There is no evading the force of the Apoſtle's words.

But the Author adds: " If it ſignifies priority in point of time, or of exiſtence, will it not be to blend Jeſus Chriſt with the maſs of creation? to make him thereby the firſt created of the works of God?" Anſwer. The Author ſeems to ſuſpect, that there is great uncertainty in his arguments: and he therefore tries to force us into his opinion by the dread of the conſequences. But the alarm is vain: and no ſuch conſequences enſue. He ſhould recollect, that the Logos, or Word of God, was not created. He was the inſtrument of the Deity, δι' ὲ και τες αιωνας εποιησεν.¹ He produced all things both *viſible, and inviſible*. Why is it imagined, that this all-productive power muſt neceſſarily be blended with the works of his own hands? How does his priority connect him with any ſubſequent matter or Being? He proceeded from the Father; but we muſt not from hence ſuppoſe, that he was firſt created, or created at all. The
Author

Author does not reflect, that the Word was united with the Deity only, and not with any finite or perishable Being, at this creation. He was not created, but begotten. Surely this is προς κεντρα λακτιζειν.

The Author goes great lengths towards his conclusion, in order to support his favourite notion. He accordingly says — p. 184 — "If the terms first-begotten, or only-begotten, had in Scripture been applied to the Λογος, the doctrine of Arius, I apprehend, ought not to have been objected to." This is surely said with too little caution. In the next page he gives a reason for his opinion, which is of a dangerous tendency. "*The doctrine of the eternal generation, if I may be permitted to speak my own opinion of it, strongly favours the cause of Arianism.*" In respect to eternal generation I can say nothing; as there is no such doctrine in Scripture: nor could I ever comprehend the notion. It seems to be an expedient devised to obviate some fancied difficulties. But suppose we were to grant, that such a

generation

generation has fubfifted, how does it at all
favour Arianifm ; in oppofition to which it
feems to have been introduced? He tells us
by an hypothefis —" For, *if* it is true, then
Chrift was always, as being a Son, fubordinate to the Father," &c. But why is it
fuppofed to be true, that, by being ftyled a
Son, he is fubordinate, or in fubjection?
This however is more than once maintained: and it is accordingly faid, that
" filiation implies inferiority." But in this
notion, I fear, that the Author attends
more to words, than to things. It is true,
in this world a helplefs child from it's birth
depends upon it's parents from it's debility,
and the nature of it's exiftence; and is for
a long time in fubfervience towards them.
But we muft not fuppofe, that this prevails
in heaven. For between the birth of a
child and the production of the Logos there
is not the leaft analogy. Therefore no juft
comparifon can be made between the relation of the Logos to the Father, and their
union; and the relation of a child to it's
earthly parent, where there is no union,
nor bodily connexion

THE AUTHOR SEEMS TO RUIN HIS OWN PURPOSE.

The Author through his whole Treatife has been trying, with much learning, and very fuccefsfully, to prove the union, and unity of the Godhead, and at the fame time the divinity of the Logos. But all this, he thinks, muft be given up, if we admit, that the original Logos, or Word, was the Son of God. As if thefe approved doctrines could be fet afide by a name, or title, or a mode of defcription. When we are told by the Evangelift — *In the beginning was the Word, and the Word was with God, and the Word was God. All things were made by him,* &c—if after this he is called *the Son of God; his firft-begotten; his only-begotten;* wherein do we find any inconfiftence? And if there be any feeming difficulty arifing from our prejudices, yet how can it make void thofe plain, and effential, truths above? We may therefore allow Chrift in his divine nature to be the Son of God, and be far removed from the notions of Arius. We need not be under any apprehenfions on that account.

5

SOME PASSAGES OUT OF MANY IN THE
NEW TESTAMENT RELATING TO THE
SECOND PERSON, WHICH DESERVE
TO BE COLLATED AND WELL
CONSIDERED.

He that fent me is with me, the Father.[1]

Neither came I of myfelf: but he fent me.[2]

*And we know, that the Son of God is come,
and hath given us underftanding, that we may
know him, that is true: and we are in him
which is true, even in his Son Jefus Chrift.
This is the true God, and eternal life.*[3]

*For unto which of the angels faid he at any
time, Thou art my Son, this day have I begotten
thee.*[4]

And

---

[1] John viii. 29.   [2] Ibid. viii. 42.

[3] I John v. 2.   [4] Heb. i. 5

And again when he (or, when he again)
bringeth his first-begotten into the world—&c.[1]

*For God sent not his Son into the world to
condemn it; but that the world through him
might be saved.*[2]

*In this was manifested the love of God
towards us, because that God sent his only-
begotten Son into the world, that we might live
through him.*[3]

*Herein is love. Not that we loved God;
but that he loved us, and sent his Son to be the
propitiation for our sins.*[4]

From these passages it appears to me
plain, that the Son of God, the only-
begotten, and first-begotten of the Father,
came from one place to another; from a
state of glory before the worlds to a state of
humiliation and subordination upon earth.

Saint

[1] Heb i. 6.　　　　[2] John iii. 17.

[3] 1 John iv. 9.　　　[4] 1 John iv. 10.

Saint Paul, fpeaking of the infufficiency of the law, tells us, that this failure was made up in Chrift.—*For what the law could not do, in that it was weak through the flefh, God, fending his own Son in the likenefs of finful flefh, and for fin, condemned fin in the flefh.*[1] We find, that Chrift in the flefh was only a likenefs of the Son of God, who was fent from heaven. — *Who being in the form of God, thought it not robbery to be equal with God; but made himfelf of no reputation, and took upon him the form of a fervant, and was made in the likenefs of man.*[2] The Son of God therefore was in the form of God, before he took upon him the likenefs of man — that is, before he was either fent, or came; before he was conceived, and took flefh. *For God fo loved the world, that he fent his only-begotten Son, that whofoever believeth in him fhould not perifh, but have everlafting life.*[3]

The

[1] Rom. viii. 3.

[2] Philip. ii. 6, 7.

[3] John iii. 16.

*The Father sent the Son to be the Saviour of
the world.*[1]

*For this purpose the Son of God was mani-
fested* (made known to mankind), *that he
might destroy the works of the devil.*[2] By
these words we may be assured, that he was
prior to his manifestation.[3]

Our Saviour is very copious upon this
subject, when he is trying to enforce upon
the Jews, that he was the Son of God, and
came down from heaven, and was in unity
with the Father. *I am not alone, but I and
the Father, that sent me.* — *Ye neither know
me, nor my Father: if ye had known me, ye
would*

---

[1] 1 John iv. 14.   [2] Ibid. iii. 8.

[3] Our Saviour does not merely say, that he was born,
raised, appointed, and introduced into the world, like
other men ; but intimates plainly, that he was antecedently sent : and his commission must have been before
his appearance. It is said, that God sent his servants,
prophets, and messengers ; Moses, Aaron, Elijah, and
others. But they all existed, before they received the
order ; and the execution was after the mandate.

would have known my Father also. — I speak to the world those things, which I have heard of him. The Jews seem to intimate, that they were sons of God through Abraham. Our Saviour answers, *I know, that ye are Abraham's seed. — I speak that which I have seen with my Father ; and ye do that which ye have seen with your Father. — They answered and said unto him, Abraham is our Father. — We be not born of fornication : we have one Father, even God. Jesus said unto them, If God were your father, you would love me ; for I proceeded forth, and came from God, (that* is, from God, my Father :) *neither came I of myself, but he sent me. I came forth from the Father, and am come into the world : again I leave the world, and go to the Father.*[1]

If he came originally from his Father, when he was sent, he must have been the Son of God, before his descent upon earth and appearance in the flesh. The filiation therefore could not have commenced at that time, when he was made man.

We

We fee in the above paffages, that our Saviour acknowledges himfelf exprefsly to be the Son of God: and he in other places affords repeated intimations of it. The people alfo from his wonderous works continually gave him that title; which he uniformly accepted and admitted. He· fpeaks of himfelf likewife as the fon of man, even when he is mentioning his divine nature, and his abode with the Father. This may be feen in the following words. *And no man hath afcended up to heaven, but he that came down from heaven; even the fon of man, which is in heaven.*[1]—This may be rendered paraphraftically in the following manner. '" No man, excepting myfelf, (whom I call the fon of man) hath ever vifited the realms of glory. For I came down from thence; and at the fame time, in refpect to my divine nature, am in heaven at this time."[2]

NOTHING

[1] 1 John iii. 13.

[2] See alfo John vi. 37, 38, 44.

NOTHING IN THE DOCTRINE REPUGNANT
TO REASON.

I am perfuaded, and have for a long time been of the opinion, that this doctrine, though abftrufe and a myftery, may, from the evidence of Scripture, be fhewn to be perfectly confonant to reafon, and by no means incomprehenfible. In what manner the operation was effected, may furpafs human apprehenfion; but the great work itfelf, as defcribed by the facred Writers, is, I think, without difficulty to be apprehended.

I believe therefore, that there is òne God from everlafting to everlafting, that is, of endlefs duration, without beginning or end; from whom all things proceeded. This is paft my comprehenfion; becaufe I cannot grafp eternity, nor have a precife knowledge of any thing infinite. But my reafon tells me moft affuredly, that there

muft

muft have been fomething through all
boundlefs duration. For (as I have elfewhere faid) if there had been originally
nothing, there could have been no produce;
no derivative either good or evil. Nothing
could have been effected, if there were no
efficient caufe: for an effect without a caufe
cannot be conceived. Being cannot proceed
from non-entity.

There muft therefore have been an original power, without beginning or end;
which was the caufe of all other beings.
The firft production of the moft High was
his Son; who proceeded from him, and
who partakes of the divine nature; and is
ftyled the firft-begotten of God, and of all
creation. By him all things were made,
that were made: all fubfequent beings were
the work of his hands, and teftify his divine
wifdom. Was then the fecond perfon co-
exiftent with the Deity? Certainly in refpect
to effence, though not as to perfonality. For
this effence, which he had as Son, was of
the fame fpiritual and eternal fubftance as

the

the Father's, before the perfonality commenced. Was then this perfonality produced
in time? Undoubtedly: for whatever is
effected, muft be brought about in time.
Some antecedent power muft produce it.
However difficult it may appear to man's
limited apprehenfion, every effect, however
remote, muft have a boundlefs duration each
way, both before, and after. An eternity
muft have paffed; and an eternity muft
enfue. Is not then the Logos to be efteemed
eternal? Not in refpect to perfonality: for
that modification took place only before
creation. But the effence, from which he
proceeded, was certainly eternal. He is
eternal from his participation of the divine
nature, which had no beginning.

Here I am obliged to differ from Dr.
Eveleigh in his excellent Difcourfe upon
this fubject, where he introduces the following words of our Saviour. [1] *And now,
O Father, glorify me with thine ownfelf, with
the*

[1] See two Sermons publifhed by him in 1791. P. 11.

the glory I had with thee before the world began. Upon which it is faid, His exifting as God with God, is here called the glory, which he had with the Father: and the time, when he had this glory, inftead of — *in the beginning*, is faid to have been — *before the world was. Both are expreſſions of the ſame extent: both imply from eternity.* He had before (page 10) faid very truly, that the divine nature was eternally poffeffed by the Son. I do not diffent in refpect to the purport, of what is here ultimately main-tained: for we both ftrive to fhew, that Chrift, as begotten of God, was in refpect to his divine effence eternal. I only pre-fume to differ in refpect to the words, and the argument, by which it is explained. For I know not how to agree in refpect to perfonality, that *in the beginning*, and *before the world was*, imply eternity. On the con-trary, they appear to me to relate to a particular time; however remote that time may have been. In confequence of this, the Son of God, and only-begotten of his Father, though of the ſame fubftance with

the

the Father, was produced at a particular period, and the perfonality had a commencement. And I think, many errors and fatal difputes have enfued from this truth not being properly obferved. I therefore repeat, that this modification of the divine nature was not, nor could be, from all eternity. When the facred Writers fpeak of the Word, as the fecond perfon, they will, I believe, be found, never to fpeak of him under that character, as from everlafting; nor fuppofe him to have thus fubfifted from all eternity. *In the beginning was the Word, and the Word was with God; and the Word was God. The fame was in the beginning with God.*[1] Eternity has no beginning. There is therefore no reference to it here. Every commencement muft be from a point; however remote and unknown that point may be. Hence we may be affured, that the Logos, or Word, was only the firft-born in refpect to fubfequent creation. Our Saviour intimates as much in his addrefs to God. — *And now, O Father,*

[1] John i. 1, 2.

Father, glorify me with thine ownself, with the glory, I had with thee (not from all eternity, but) *before the world was.*[1] In conformity to this St. Paul mentions him, as — *the image of the invisible God; the first-born of every creature: for by him were all things created.*[2] And he is styled by St. John — *the beginning of the creation of God: and the Lamb slain from the foundation of the world.*[3] *A Lamb without blemish, and without spot: who verily was fore-ordained before the foundation of the world.*[4] — *Who hath saved, and called us with an holy calling; not according to our own works; but according to his own purpose and grace; which was given us in Christ Jesus, before the world began.*[5] Our Saviour, when he supplicates for his own Disciples, says — *Father, I will,* or request, *that they may behold my glory, which thou hast given me: for thou lovedst me before the foun-*
                                                        dation

---

[1] John xvii. 5.   [2] Coloss. i. 15.

[3] Revelat. iii. 14. and xiii. 8.   [4] 1 Pet. i. 19, 20.

[5] 2 Tim. i. 9.

dation of the world.[1] This is the terminus, to which the Logos, or fecond Perfon, feems to be uniformly referred, as being antecedent to all created beings; and of a more exalted nature, and divine origin; even from God himfelf immediately, and confubftantial with him.

But we find a different mode of expreffion ufed, when the facred Writers fpeak of God; who is reprefented by them as through all eternity, without beginning, as well as without end. *From everlafting to everlafting thou art God.*[2] *Thy throne is of old: thou art from everlafting.*[3] *Art not thou from everlafting, O Lord, my God?*[4] The Prophet Ifaiah alfo mentions the Deity in a very fublime manner — *The lofty One, that inhabiteth eternity.*[5] The mode of addrefs is remarkable; and fhews, wherein the two

great

[1] John xvii. 24.   [2] Pfalm xc. 2.

[3] Pfalm xciii. 2,   [4] Habak. i. 12.

[5] Ifai a Vii 1

great objects differ. God is felf-exiftent, independent, and has exifted through a boundlefs duration. The Son, as a Perfon, proceeded from the Father, and was produced in time; yet is eternal, as a derivative from God and a portion of the divine Nature; and at all times *in the bofom of the Father*, that is, in ftrict union with him. *I and the Father are one.*

THE NOTION OF ETERNAL GENERATION AGAIN CONSIDERED.

They, who entertain the notion of an eternal generation, feem to be mifled by a term, of which they can have no determinate knowledge. It was introduced merely as an help towards folving a fuppofed difficulty, which, I think, never exifted. In fhort it is a greater myftery, than that, which it is brought to explain. A perfon might juft as reafonably infift upon an eternal creation: and it would appear to many equally plaufible. But at this rate it

would

would be found, that the world was formed by divine wifdom, and yet never had a beginning: which is as abfurd, as it is untrue. They remove the object, as far as they can, out of fight, in order to have a better view. But the whole is a fallacy. · It is therefore idle in them, like the fchoolmen formerly, to make ufe of terms without any precife purport, more efpecially words of no meaning at all, to explain, what they do not comprehend. We can never obtain light by returning into darknefs: nor remedy one difficulty by introducing another much greater.

This is verified in the doctrine mentioned above concerning eternal generation: which feems calculated to perplex rather than inftruct, and implies a contradiction. We have feen, that the Logos proceeded from God, and was begotten of the Father. But how could he have been begotten, or have proceeded, if he never had a beginning? Who firft produced this mode of argument, I know not: but it feems to be founded in mere metaphyfical fophiftry.

AN

AN OBJECTION STATED.

It may be afked, *Why may not there be an eternal generation of the Son, as well an everlafting duration of the Father? Has not God exifted through all eternity?* The Deity moft certainly has ever exifted, and will endure for ever. But there is a great and irreconcileable difference between thefe two articles: and we therefore cannot form any juft analogy between them. The great, everlafting, and felf-exifting God owes not his being to any power, or to any antecedent caufe: for it is to the laft degree abfurd to fuppofe any thing antecedent to what is eternal. There was therefore no operation in his produſtion; for he was not produced; being, as was before obferved, felf-exiftent, and prior to all things. But in refpeſt to the Word of God, the Logos, in his produſtion there was an . antecedent purpofe, and an operation. He was begotten of the Father; which intimates a faſt:

and

---

and as I before afferted, and I think paft contradiction, every fact muft have been compleated in time. Hence it is faid — *this day have I begotten thee :* which plainly proves, that the operation could not be otherwife than in time. This is farther intimated in the addrefs of our Saviour to God, when he fays — *And now, O Father, glorify thou me with thine own felf with the glory, which I had with thee, before the world was.*[1] He does not fay, the glory, which I had always, through all eternity, but only antecedent to Creation. When this was accomplifhed, we know not: we only learn thus far, that previous to all things created Chrift was begotten of his Father; and that then began the filiation. Hence we may accede to the words in the Nicene Creed, where thefe doctrines are very juftly fet forth, and demand our attention and belief. " I believe in God. . . . . And in one Lord Jefus Chrift, the only begotten Son of God: Begotten of the Father before all worlds: God

---

[1] John xvii. 5.

God of God: Light of Light: Very God of very God: Begotten, not made: Being of one fubftance with the Father: By whom all things were made." The fame as the Father, and eternal, in refpect to effence and original divinity; but pofteriour in refpect to filiation and adoption: which adoption and filiation muft have been in time.

I therefore think, that they, who apply to an eternal generation, run into very unneceffary difficulties, not to fay abfurdities. For they fuppofe a fact to be accomplifhed without a beginning; a wonderful operation without any primary efficient caufe; that is, without an operator: which is impoffible. This trouble is, I fay, needlefs; as every thing mentioned in Scripture about the Logos, or Word of God, may be more clearly proved upon much better principles.

R

SOME WRONG NOTIONS STATED AND CONFUTED.

A Writer of note[1] has afforded repeated instances of his diffent from the Church of England in refpect to thefe articles. In his addrefs to the difciples of Swedenborg, he fpeaks of them with unwarrantable keennefs and deteftation. He tells them, p. 2. that he is of their opinion, and looks with *equal horror* upon thefe doctrines of the Trinity, as equally *abfurd and blafphemous, conftituting in fact three Gods.* Yet he muft have known, that, according to the articles of the Church, which he condemns, one God only is acknowledged. Of the perfonality and divine nature of our Saviour I have faid a great deal; and have particularly dwelt upon that decifive declaration, when he faid — *I and the Father are one.* The Jews

[1] Dr. Priefley. See Letters to the Members of the New Jerufalem Church, publifhed in 1791.

Jews immediately infifted, that he made himfelf equal with God; and taxed him with blafphemy. In his anfwer he admits the words, and the character, which he had affumed: but denies, that there was either blafphemy, or prefumption.[1]

As to the Logos proceeding from God, and partaking of his divine nature, I cannot fee any thing in it more difficult to be believed, than in the conception and generation of man, or in the production of the fruits in the field. The operation, whether in earth, or in heaven, is alike myfterious to me, and paft my comprehenfion. Yet I muft give up my fenfes, if I believe not the one; and my reafon and religion, if I deny the other: for it is tranfmitted to me under the higheft fanction, and the moft unqueftionable authority. If there be any difficulty, it arifes from wrong reafoning.
For,

[1] John x. 36.

For, as I have before intimated, can it be more extraordinary for God in his infinite wifdom and power to produce from himfelf a Divinity, the exprefs image of his perfon and brightnefs, than for an animal by blind inftinct to create the fimilitude of it-felf, and produce it's own fpecies ? It may be faid, that both the inftinct and the pro-duction are ultimately from God. It is very true. Why then do we prefume in any refpect to limit the Almighty; and think, that to Omnipotence one operation is more difficult than another ?

CONCERNING

CONCERNING MELCHIZEDEC KING OF
SALEM.

It is faid, upon the return of Abram
from *the flaughter of Chedorlaomer, and the
four Kings in the valley of Shavah*, that
*Melchizedek, King of Salem, who was the
prieft* alfo *of the moft High God, brought forth
bread and wine, and bleffed Abram, and faid:
Bleffed be Abram of the moft High God, pof-
feffor of Heaven and Earth: And bleffed be
the moft High God, which hath delivered thine
enemies into thy hand*—And that *he* (Abram)
gave him tithes of all.[1]

There have been a variety of conjectures
concerning this paffage and a diverfity of
opinions; which, I think, if we confider
the context, and the words of the Apoftle
St. Paul, will be found by no means obfcure, and attended with no great difficulty.
It

[1] Genefis xiv. 18, 19, 20.

It is well known, that it pleafed God to manifeſt himſelf to the Patriarchs, and Pro-phets of old, by a perſonage, whom the Jews looked upon as their Jehovah. He was at times ſtyled the Angel of God, the Angel of the Lord, the Angel of the preſence; the Angel, that redeemed Jacob from evil; the fame, whom God was pleaſed to promiſe, that he would ſend before his ſervants; and who is by Malachi ſtyled the Angel of the Covenant. He is ſaid in the paſſage above to have been the Prieſt of the moſt High God. And by his appearance before Abram he gave the Patriarch an intimation of Chriſt, the High Prieſt to come; and of the myſtic bread and wine, which would one day be inſtituted by him. By the Apoſtle St. Paul we are told, that this great Perſonage was *without father, without mother; without deſcent; having neither beginning of days, nor end of life.*[1] Hence it is manifeſt, that this could be no other, than the divine Logos; that is, a
reprefentation

reprefentation of him under a human form: and it is *accordingly faid of him*, that *he was made like unto the Son of God*, an image of Chrift to come.[1]

All this would have appeared very plain, had it not been for a miftake, which has prevailed in almoft all the tranflations; and was firft introduced by the Authors of the greek Verfion. The words in the original are Melchi zedec, and Melech Salem. Thefe, though two of them are fomewhat diverfified, fignify *the King of righteoufnefs*, and *the King of peace*. This is well known: and we have the additional authority of St. Paul, who was a good judge of their meaning.[2] Now the two firft terms are retained in the verfions without any interpretations; and the two other terms are partly tranflated, and partly left, as in the original. The latter is in our Verfion rendered— *The King of Salem*; which Salem is generally

fuppofed

---

[1] Heb. vii. 3.   [2] Ibid. vii. 2.

fuppofed to fignify Jerufalem. It is incon-
ceivable, what obfcurity has been brought
upon the hiftory by the words, which are
fufficiently plain in the original, being thus
left without an explication; and by the
character and office of the perfon being
thus introduced, as a proper name. For
by thefe means one of his attributes is
reprefented, as a name of a Canaanitifh
place.

It may be worth while to take notice of
the falfe gloffes, which have hence enfued;
and the inconfiftences, which have been
maintained. In the firft place, as the words
Melchi zedec have been admitted as a proper
name of a man, many have taken much
pains to find out, who that man could
have been. Jerome fays, ¹ that he was fuppofed to have been Shem the fon of Noah.
But who can believe, that the Patriarch
Shem, if he were ever a King, fhould have
reigned in the idolatrous region of Canaan?
According

According to the Author of the Chronicon Pafchale,[1] he was of the race of Ham. This is equally incredible, that any body of the line of Ham fhould be a Prieft of the moft High God. Suidas goes upon the fame principle, and tells us, that he was the fon of Side, the fon of Ægyptus, King of Libya; that he was himfelf King of Canaan, and reigned in Jerufalem, called Salem. He fays farther, that he was King of the Jews, and (εκ Ιεδαιων μονον) not only of the Jews, but of the Gentiles in general: and all this in the time of Abram; and before Abram had any child. There was hardly ever fuch a complication of abfurdities. How could a fon of Side, or a fon of Ham, or a fon of Noah, be a perfon, who had *neither father nor mother*; *who was of no defcent*; *and had neither beginning of days, nor end of life?* And how could he reign over the Jews, before any of the family of Judah, or of Jacob, were in being?

The

[1] P. 49, 50.

The like miftakes occur concerning
Salem, which is reprefented, as a city.
Jofephus fays, that Melchizedec reigned
there; and that it was the fame as Solyma,
which was afterward called Jerufalem. [1]
This is a great miftake; for it was called
Jerufalem, before the Ifraelites were in pof-
feffion of it: and the name is continually
repeated quite through the Scriptures. [2] And
what is very extraordinary, it was never
called Solyma: at leaft the name does not
once occur in the Sacred Writings, neither
in the Original, nor in the greek Verfion. It
was a name formed by the Greeks afterwards; who changed Ἱερεσαλημ to Ἱεροσολυμα; and who would perfuade the world,
that it was compounded, and formed from
the greek word Ἱερος and Solyma. The
fame is obfervable in the etymology of the
former name; which has been in like manner by fome deduced from Ἱερος and Σαλημ.

It

[1] Ant. lib. i. c. viii. p. 32.

[2] See Jofhua, x. 1. and Judges, i. 21. It is called
Jeruf' t.

It is accordingly faid in the Etymologicum
Magnum — *Jerufalem was firft called Salem;
but, when Chrift made his appearance there,
it was named* ¹ Ἰερȣ-σαλημ, *the holy City of
Salem.* Hence we learn, to what a degree
of abfurdity people will go.

But there is not an inftance in Scripture
of Salem being put for Jerufalem, excepting
in thofe paffages in Genefis, where it is fo
rendered by a great miftake. The only
place, where it feems to have been efteemed
a proper name, is in fome verfions of the
feventy fixth Pfalm, v. 2. where it is faid —
*In Judah is God known — and his tabernacle
is in Salem.* But here the ancient Greek
Verfion² differs, and gives the fenfe more
truly — και εγεννηθη εν ειρηνη ὁ τοπος αυτȣ —
And his place (of refidence) *was made, or
founded*

---

¹ —— ιλθων ὁ Χϛιϛος ιις αυτην ικλνθη Ἰερȣσαλημ. Theophilus has been guilty of the fame miftake. — Ἰερȣσαλημ,
ἡ σροειϛημιεν Ἰεροσολυμα, Ad. Autol. L. ii. p. 372. Edit.
Benedict.

² In this Verfion fee Pfalm lxxv. 2.

founded in peace. Analogous to this are the words in Job. *Know, thy tabernacle shall be in peace.*[1] *The kingdom of God is peace.*[2] *The very God of peace sanctify you wholly.*[3] The Apostle speaking concerning this very controverted passage in Genesis says, *the King of Salem, that is, the King of peace.*[4] And this interpretation is allowed by Suidas, and by every writer, who has given a solution of it, however inconsistent in other respects.

Jerome was aware, that by Salem could not be meant Jerusalem: but he was still persuaded, that it was the name of a city; and (strange to tell) that Melchizedec reigned there. He supposes it to have been the same as Salim near Bethsan, called afterwards Scythopolis: it was also thought to be near Ænon, where John baptized. [5] Salem oppidum est juxta Scythopolim, quod

[1] Job v. 24
[2] Rom. xiv. 17.
[3] 1 Thess. v. 23.
[4] Heb. vii. 2.

[5] Epistola ad Evagrium de Melchizedec. Vol. ii p. 570.

quod ufque hodie appellatur Salem : et oftenditur illic Palatium Melchizedec, ex magnitudine ruinarum veteris operis oftendens magnificentiam. Let this palace, which muft have exifted in the time of Abraham, have been ever fo fplendid, and it's ruins as magnificent, as Jerome would perfuade us, yet we may be well affured, that Melchizedec never reigned there. It is, I think, manifeft, that there was never any man fo called; nor was Salem a proper name. This account of Jerome is void of all truth, and fupported by no authority. What he mentions of Salim, others refer to Sion, juft as fancy directs — Εν τω ορει τω λεγομενω Σιων. Suidas.

I have mentioned that Melchi zedec fignifies *the King of Righteoufnefs*: and, I believe, it is never in the Scriptures given as a name to any earthly Monarch ; but to God only. Hence it is faid by Jeremiah — *This is his name, The Lord our righteoufnefs.*'

The

' Jeremiah xxiii. 6.

The Lord of Hofts, the King of glory, the Sun of righteounefs, the Branch of rightcoufnefs, were all Sacred titles. It is fometimes rendered JUSTICE. And it is faid, *A King fhall reign in juftice:* And God is continually reprefented as a God of all juftice and truth. Hence Jeremiah fays, *The Lord is the God of truth.*[1]

In like manner Melech Salem, *the King of peace*, was a title, which could not well be given to any Prince of the earth. It feems to be confined folely to the Deity. He is accordingly ftyled *the God of peace.*[2] *The God of peace ..... make you perfect:*[3] *The very God of peace fanctify you wholly.*[4] And of the Meffiah faith a Prophet— *His name fhall be called ... The Prince of Peace.*[5]

However

[1] Jeremiah x. 10.   [2] Rom. xv. 33.

[3] Heb. xiii. 20.   [4] 1 Theff. v. 23.

[5] Ifaiah ix. 7.

However in refpect to Melchizedec, a learned ¹Friend·fuggefted to me, that there is an inftance of a man being called after this manner. This is to be found in the name Adoni·zedec, *the Lord of juftice*; by which a King of Canaan in the days of Jofhua was denominated. There is certainly a perfect analogy between them; but with fome difference. For we fee, that the Perfon, with whom Abram had an interview, was not only defcribed as the King *of juftice*, or *righteoufnefs*; but alfo as the Prince *of Peace:* which renders the character more particular and extraordinary. I believe therefore, that I may ftill venture to fay, that no mortal was fo highly diftinguifhed. Add to this, as I have obferved before, that thefe marks of diftinction, as applied above, are not properly names, but fignificant and prophetic titles. They belong to a divine Perfonage, and are peculiar to his character, whofe kingdom was to be founded in righteoufnefs and maintained in peace.

We

¹ Rev. Mr. Peter Roberts of Eton.

We may therefore be affured, that this grand Perfonage, who appeared to Abram, and who was *without beginning of days, and end of life, alfo without defcent,* could be no other than the Divine Logos, or Word of God. They were therefore both the fame divine Perfon under a fimilar appearance, but at two different times. The former reprefentation in a human form was introduced to give Abram fome intimation of the real everlafting High Prieft to come; of whom the former was merely a temporary type: for, though antecedent, he is faid expreflly *to be made like unto the Son of God.* Hence he, as well as the latter, is faid — *to abide a Prieft continually,* or for ever.[r]

I fhould therefore think, that the account given by Mofes might be rendered in the following manner.

And the King of rightcoufnefs, (the fame as) *the Prince of peace, brought forth bread and wine; and he was a Prieft of the moft High God.*

And

[r] Heb. vii. 3.

And he bleſſed him and ſaid, Bleſſed be Abram of the moſt High God; poſſeſſor of Heaven and Earth.

And bleſſed be the moſt High God, which hath delivered thine enemies into thy hand: and he (Abram) *gave him tithes of all;* that is, of all his ſpoil, which he had taken from the four Kings.

St. Paul could have explained more clearly this wonderful hiſtory, if he had thought proper to ſpeak out, and to have afforded the intelligence in his power. But he had a prejudiced people to deal with; who had entertained a preconceived opinion. And we may continually perceive a very wiſe mode of proceeding, which the Apoſtles obſerved, and their great Maſter before them. This was, never to enter into any cavil about the rendering of names; nor about any popular notions of the Jews; when theſe notions did not interfere with the truth; and when the Goſpel, which

S they

they preached, was not injured by their acquiefcence. They never regarded, whether it was Balaam the fon of Beor, or of Bozar; whether it was Jofhua, or Jefus; Elijah or Elias; Eleazar or Lazarus; Quirinus, or Cyrenius; Ἱερυσαλημ or Ἱεροσολυμα. They mentioned fuch names, as were in ufe among the people, to whom they addreffed themfelves, and as were beft underftood. Hence St. Paul acquiefces in Melchizedec being admitted as a proper name, becaufe it was fo efteemed by the Hebrews, to whom he wrote. Yet he intimates plainly, that it ought properly to be otherwife underftood : for the purport of the hiftory depended upon the true interpretation. And if fo, the words, of which thofe pretended names were compofed, fhould be accordingly inter-preted, and thus admitted for the fake of edification.

As to the bread and wine, which were brought forth to Abram by this Prieft of God, they were not offered, as Jofephus, and

and Philo maintained, and as Grotius, Le
Clerc, and others, have fince fuppofed, for
the refrefhment of his little army: for he
had enough, and to fuffice. He had refufed
to accept, what the King of Sodom had
tendered; and had likewife given tithes of
all he had taken: which implies abundance.
The bread and wine, thus offered by this
great Prieft, were fignificant emblems of the
like offerings enjoined afterwards by Chrift;
which he ordained as a myfterious refemblance of his body and blood. And this,
we may fuppofe, Abram was made to underftand; as the whole was intended to give
him an infight into the bleffings to come.

I am not unfupported in what I fay; for
this was an opinion of old — Melchizedeck
in typo Chrifti panem et vinum obtulit; et
myfterium Chriftianum in Salvatoris fan-
guine et corpore dedicavit. [1]

Melchifedeck

---

[1] Paulæ et Euftoch. Epift. apud Hieron. Vol. iv.
p. 547.

Melchifedeck facrificio panis et vini
myfterium Dominici corporis et fanguinis
expreffit.[1]

Μελχισεδεκ, Βασιλευς ειρηνης, ὁ Ἰερευς τε Θεε
τε ὑψιςε, ὁ τον οινον και τον αρτον την ἡγιασ-
μενην διδες τροφην, εις τυπον ευχαριςιας. και δη
ἑρμηνευεται ὁ Μελχισεδεκ, Βασιλευς δικαιος.
Συνωνυμια δε εςι δικαιοσυνης και ειρηνης.[2]

As Melchi zedec, *the King of Righteoufnefs* was the forerunner, and type, of *the
Lord of Righteoufnefs, the Holy one*, and *the
Juft one*; we fhall find all, that was faid of
his Priefthood, fulfilled in Chrift — We
learn particularly from St. Paul, that it was
accomplifhed. Hence it is faid — *We have
a great High Prieft, who is paffed into the
heavens, Jefus the Son of God.* [3] Again
whither

---

[1] Incerti — ad Demetriadem Virginem Epift. apud
Hieron. Vol. v. p. 14.

[2] Clem. Alexand. Strom. Lib. iv. p. 637.

[3] H

whither (into which heavens) *the forerunner is for us entered, even Jesus, made an High Priest after the order* (not of Levi, nor of any mortal, but) *of Melchi zedec,* the Prince of Righteousness. *We have such an High Priest, who is set on the right hand of the throne of the Majesty in the heavens.*[2] He is *made an High Priest for ever.*[3] And the former High Priest, who was seen by Abram, was formed after his likeness.[4]

Hence I think, that the passage in St. Paul's Epistle, where he is particularly describing the Person, of whom we have been treating, may be explained in the following manner.

[5]*For this person, whom you call Melchisedec, the King of Salem, Priest of the most High God, who met Abram returning from the*
                                        slaughter

---

[1] Heb. vi. 20.   [2] Ibid. viii. 1.

[3] Heb. vi. 20.   [4] Ibid. vii. 3.

[5] Heb. vii. v.

*flaughter of the kings, and bleffed him; to whom
alfo Abram gave a tenth part of all* (his fpoils
and booty;) *firft being by interpretation, the
King of Righteoufnefs, and after that alfo King
of Salem, which is the King of peace,* (two
fignificant titles, and not properly names)
*being alfo without father, without mother,
without defcent, having neither beginning of
days, nor end of life,* (confequently not
mortal, nor having any relation to the fons
of men) *but made like unto the Son of God*;
(the prior being made in conformity to the
latter, and therefore, alius et idem, the very
Logos in a human form, and a reprefentation of Chrift, who was to come in the
flefh) This Perfon, I fay, *like the Son of
God,* and the very Son of God, *abideth a
Prieft continually.*[1]

It is from this defcription, that I have
been induced to affert, that this King of
Righteoufnefs, who appeared to Abram in a
human fhape, was the Word of God, called
alfo

[1] Heb. vii. 1 - 3

alfo Jehovah, and the Angel of the Lord. He was the fame in refpect to heavenly effence as the Logos, or Word of God; and his reprefentative in a bodily form. Hence our Saviour is defcribed by the Prophets, as *a righteous Branch*: as *a King who was to reign, and profper*; and *whofe name was to be the Lord our Righteoufnefs.*[1] He was accordingly in a more permanent manner manifefted in the flefh; and maintained the character, to which he was appointed. Thus we find, that for the underftanding of thefe truths it is neceffary, that the terms, of which we have been treating, fhould be literally tranflated, and not left as proper[2] names undefined,

---

[1] Jerem. xxiii. 5, 6. Ifaiah xxxii. 1.

[2] I am fenfible, that, to fubftitute titles or attributes in the room of names, may appear uncouth, efpecially to an ear, which has been otherwife habituated. But to fay, that the King of Righteoufnefs met Abram is not a whit more ftrange, than if we were to fay — The Lord of Righteoufnefs met Abram — The Lord of Juftice will avenge — The God of Peace will comfort — The Lord of Hofts will go forth — The Angels of the Lord met him. Gen. xxxii. 1.

undefined, though they are in fome degree, and for good reafons, thus admitted by St. Paul.

For I am perfuaded, as I have intimated before, that the Apoftle in his account of this paffage of the Mofaic hiftory was unwilling to combat the popular opinion of the Jews. He therefore ufes a proper precaution, that he may not give unneceffary offence; and at the fame time difcovers the truth. He accordingly affords a juft character of the divine Perfon, who appeared, at two intervals; and fhews, *who he was*, without declaring, *who he was not*: which however is made apparent from his precife and fignificant defcription.

CONCERNING A MODE OF EXPLANATION
USED BY SOME MISSIONARIES.

It is faid of the Spanifh Miffionaries in America, that, when they would explain the divine hypoftafis, they for an emblem make ufe of the figure of a tree with two branches, to fhew, that unity is confiftent with degrees of partition, and perfonality. Hence by a proper analogy they propofe, and afterwards folve, all the objections, and difficulties, by this defcription of the type, which have at times been raifed in refpect to the primary object, alluded to under this reprefentation. They therefore afk, if this ftately Tree be one or more : and it is anfwered, that there are certainly three portions, divided, but not feparated, being in ftrict union, Three in One. If it be objected by thofe, to whom they addrefs themfelves, that then the con-verfe muft likewife be true, and One muft be Three, which implies a contradiction; this is over-ruled by the object delineated

before

before their eyes, where they fee to a de-
monftration, that Unity may be dilated to
Plurality, and the connexion, and union
preferved. They are farther taught, that
two of the portions are derivatives, which
are thus in ftrict union with the Tree itfelf;
and remain firmly connected, and in fome
degree embodied, though diverfified in refpect to order and deftination. They are
therefore co-exiftent with the parent Tree:
for they are of the fame original with the
body from the firft, though pofterior in
refpect to their protrufion, and divifion,
and they form collectively one and the fame
object.

CONCERNING SOME VERY CURIOUS DOC-
TRINES OF THE ANCIENT CHINESE,

TAKEN FROM

MEMOIRES CONCERNANT L'HISTOIRE, &C.
CHINOIS PAR LES MISSIONAIRES DE
PEKIN. 1776. TOM. I.

ALSO FROM

THE ANCIENT CHOU-KING. A PARIS 1770.

I have mentioned, that the Jews had certainly traces of the Supreme Hypoftafis; that their Jehovah, the Angel of the Covenant, was no other than the fecond Perfon in that Triad; that he under the Father was the great operator in the work of creation; that he appeared to their Fathers; and that they looked up to him as their guardian Deity. They were likewife not ignorant of the Holy Spirit, which co-operated in all things, *by which God garnifhed the heavens. Thou fendeft forth thy Spirit, and they are created: and thou renewest the face of*
the

the earth.[1] With thefe firft principles of divine knowledge the Jews were of old acquainted : and thefe, together with other intelligence from the Hiftory of Mofes, I imagine, they brought into China, when they at times were admitted into that country, particularly into the province of Honan. Their admiffion may have been not long after their firft captivity. Though fome of the articles may not be quite to my prefent purpofe, yet I will not omit them ; as they will, I believe, prove very fatisfactory to the Reader.

Some of thefe extracts are taken from the Chinefe hiftorian Lo-pi, who lived in the Dynafty of Song, about eight hundred years ago. But the books, to which he applied for intelligence, and from which he quotes, are of far more early date. They are of the higheft antiquity, and are faid to have been written many ages before the Chriftian Æra.

Others

---

[1] Pfalm civ. 30.

Others are taken from the Chou-king, which is efteemed to be the moft facred book among the Chinefe; and is held in the fame reverence, as the Pentateuch of Mofes is among the Jews; and fuppofed to be of greater antiquity. The book L' Y-king, and Ta-tchouen are as old as Confucius, who was five hundred years before Chrift.

What I have mentioned, that the Spanifh Miffionaries exprefs by a tree with two arms, the Chinefe of old reprefented by an emblem which bears a ftrong analogy to it. This was a figure like the Greek Upfilon, Y, which they called u, or rather y. And the book, in which the myftery is explained, has the name of L' Y-king —*the Book of* Y: which is extraordinary.

²Lo-pi dit, qu' il a connu par L' Y-king dans l' article Ta-tchouen (L' Y-king eft le nom du plus ancien, du plus obfcur, et du plus eftimé de tous les monuments,

que

¹ Chou-king. Difcours Preliminaire, p. xLv.
² Note 2. Ibid.

que le Chine nous ait confervès) *que le Ciel et la Terre ont un commencement.* Et il ajoûte, *que, fi cela fe dit de la Terre et du Ciel, à plus forte raifon doit-il fe dire de l' Homme.*

Dans le chapitre [1]Su-koua, (un autre petit Traité, qu'on trouve dans le même livre) on parle forte clairement de l' origine du monde. *Après qu'il y eut un Ciel et une Terre,* dit le texte, *toutes les chofes matérielles furent formées : Enfuit il y eut le male et la femelle ; puis le mari et la femme, &c.*

[2]Dans le Hi-tfe (ce qui Lo-pi a appellé cì deffu Ta-tchouen) on lit ces paroles. *L' Y poffede le Grand Terme.* ——— Lo-pi expliquant cet endroit du Hi-tfe dit, que *le Grand Terme eft la Grande Unité et le Grand Y : que l' Y n' a ni corps ni figure : et que tout ce, qui a corps et figure, a été fait par ce, qui n' a ni figure ni corps.*

La

[1] Page xlv. Su-koua, un autre petit Traité, dont on fait Confucius Auteur.

[2] Ib

[1] La tradition port, que *le Grand Terme ou la Grand Unitè comprends Trois: qu' Un eſt Trois; et que Trois ſont Un.*

[2] Le charactere Y, dit Vang-chin, *ne marque point ici un livre nommé* Y: *mais il faut ſcavoir, que au commencement, quand il n' y avoit point encore de Grand Terme, dès-lors exiſtoit une raiſon agiſſante et inépuiſable, qui aucune image ne peut repréſenter, qui aucun nom ne peut nommer, qui eſt infinie en toutes manieres, et à laquelle on ne peut rien ajoûter.*

OF THE POWER STYLED TAO.

[3] Tao eſt vie; *le premier a engendré le ſecond; les deux ont produit le troiſieme; les trois ont faites toutes choſes. Celui, qui l' eſprit apperçoit, et qui l' œil ne peut voir, ſe nomme* Y.

LETTRE

---

[1] Chou-king. Diſcours Preliminaire, p. XLVI.

[2] Ibid. p. XLVII.

[3] Memoire- C⋯ ⋯ . V⋯ ⋯ ⋯

LETTRE SUR LES CARACTERES CHINOIS.
A PEKIN. 1776.

¹Parmi les anciens Caracteres Chinois,
qui ont eté confervés, on trouve celui-ci △.
Selon le Dictionaire de Kang-hi, ce caractere
fignifie Union. Ecoutons les Chinois fur fon
analyfe. Selon le Choue-ouen, ce livre fi
vanté, △ *eft trois unis en un.* — Lieou-chou-
tfing hoen, qui eft une explication rai-
fonée et fcavante des plus anciens Caracteres
s'exprime ainfi. △ *fignifie union intime,*
harmonie, le premier bien de l'homme, du
ciel, et de la terre. C'eft l'union des trois
Tfai. (Tfai fignifie principe, puiffance, habilité,
dans le Tao :) car unis, ils dirigent enfemble,
créent, et nouriffent. L'image 丰 *(trois unis*
en une feule figure) n'eft pas fi obfcure en
elle même: cependant il eft difficile d'en
raifonner fans fe tromper, il n'eft pas aifé
d'en parler. Je connois la délicateffe de
                                    notre

¹ M

notre fiècle, et la rigueur de plus fages
Critiques, dès qu'il s'agit de Religion.
Malgré cela, J'ofe conjecturer, que le
caractere Δ pouroit avoir eté chez les
anciens Chinois le fymbole de la très-
adorable Trinité. — On trouve dans les
anciens livres une foule de textes, qui font
croire, que les anciens Chinois connoiffoient
ce grand myftere. Le livre Sée-ki dit,
Autrefois l'Empereur facrifioit folemnellement
de trois en trois ans a l'Efprit, Trinité en
unité — *Chin-San-ye.*

[2]Hiu-chin a vécu fou la Dynaftie du
Han, entre l'an 209 avant J. C. et l'an 190
après J. C. [3]Hiu-chin, expliqûant le caractere Y, dit ces paroles. *Au premier*
commencement La Raifon (the Λογος of Philo
and the Scriptures) *fubfiftoit dans l'unité;*
c'eft elle, qui fit et divifa le Ciel et la
Terre, convertit et perfectionna toutes chofes.

I clofe

---

[1] Memoires Chinois, V. i. p. 299, 300.

[a] Note 3. Chou-king, p. XLIX.

[3] Chou-king, ibid.

T

I clofe with one more reference to the Memoires Chinois, V. i. p. 105.

'La création du Monde et de l'Homme, l'etat d'innocence, la chûte d'Adam, et la longue vie des premiers hommes, font arti- culés auffi clairement, qu'on peut le defirer dans nos anciennes Chroniques. *Celui, qui eft lui-meme fon principe, et fa racine,* dit Tchouan-tféc, *a fait le Ciel, et la Terre.*

I have mentioned, that this intelligence may have poffibly been obtained from fome Jews of the difperfion. From whatever fource it was derived, the hiftory is very extraordinary.

THE END.

E R R A T A.

Pagf 15. note			μεταωρος	μετεωρος
69. l. 2	} for {	eundum	} read {	eundem,
73. l. 3.		δευτερον		δευτερον
155.		xxx		xxxix

Lightning Source UK Ltd.
Milton Keynes UK
UKHW020351050122
396630UK00003B/141